Studies on the Chinese Market Economy Series

Reforming China's Financial System

Chief Editors:
Gao Shangquan *and* Chi Fulin
Written by:
Zhu Huayou

FOREIGN LANGUAGES PRESS   BEIJING

First Edition 1996

The project is aided by
Hainan (China) Foundation for Reform and Development Research.

ISBN 7-119-01341-6

© Foreign Languages Press, Beijing, China, 1996

Published by Foreign Languages Press
24 Baiwanzhuang Road, Beijing 100037, China

Distributed by China International Book Trading Corporation
35 Chegongzhuang Xilu, Beijing 100044, China
P.O. Box 399, Beijing, China

Printed in the People's Republic of China

Preface

Since the goals of socialist market economy were defined at 14th National Congress of the Communist Party of China in 1992, China has accelerated its reform of economic system and entered a stage of overall deepening of the reform. As a major component of reforming the economic system, reform in financial system has become of key importance, significant in the overall reform of the economic system.

The Academy of China (Hainan) Reform and Development has, in recent years, paid great attention to the study of reforming the financial system, forming special groups to study related subjects and put forward their findings and suggestions.

At the end of 1991, the State Commission for Restructuring the Economy, the People's Bank of China, the World Bank and the UN Development Program jointly convened an international seminar on China's financial reform at the Academy of China (Hainan) Reform and Development. More than 60 senior economic management expert officials and financial experts from China's mainland, Taiwan region, the Republic of South Korea, Japan, Malaysia, Thailand, Britain, the World Bank, the International Monetary Fund and the UN Development Program made a profound study on the subject of how to deepen the reform of China's financial system.

This book collects together these study reports prepared by the Academy of China (Hainan) Reform and Development and the important study results achieved at the international seminar, and incorporates the results of financial studies made by Chinese experts in recent years. Sincere thanks go to both Chinese and foreign experts.

The book explores in depth the contradictions and outstanding questions arising through the reform of financial system and operation of financial mechanism, and puts forward some specific opinions and programs. It explores and fully discusses many questions, and presents the various ideas, viewpoints and suggestions on these questions held by Chinese and foreign experts to the reader, who can gain greater understanding through comparison and judgment.

Contents

Chapter *I*
Seize Opportunity and Boldly Promote Financial Reform

The 14th National Congress of the Communist Party of China in 1992 clearly stated the goal of China's economic system reform—the establishment of socialist market economic system. This goal is essentially the method of developing a commodity economy by allocating social resources on the basis of market mechanisms and the transformation process of replacing the method of allocating social resources mainly based on the planned economy which is characterized by administrative orders. As the financial mechanism is an organic component of market mechanisms, its structural changes and functional evolution form a major link in this transformation process.

The allocation of resources by market is, first of all, the allocation of monetary capital and the results of financing directly affect the efficiency of resources allocation. Socialist market economy needs a sound and rational financial system; otherwise, the market-based allocation of resources becomes meaningless. To meet the needs of developing a socialist market economy, therefore, it is imperative to accelerate China's financial system reform and establish the financial system that conforms with the operation of a market economy. Guided by Comrade Deng Xiaoping's talks during his inspection tour in the south and the CPC 14th National Congress, China's reform, opening to the outside world and modernization drive have entered a new stage of vigorous development since 1992. The whole nation witnessed an unprecedented high tide of construction and a number of places achieved high-speed or even very high-speed development; the general situation is good. To promote this excellent situation, financial situation is good. To promote this excellent situation, financial organizations contributed much beneficial work. The main problems at the present time are: the rapid increase of national investment in fixed assets, the rather large amount of money in circulation, the price rises of some means of production by broad margins, and the growing pressure exerted by inflation. There are many causes contributing to this situation, and it is also closely related to finance. The question of general concern is, while promoting economic development, how to strengthen state macroeconomic control and establish the new order of a socialist market economy.

The present economic regulation and control by the state mainly encompass the fields of the loan amounts, or the scale of capital construction, interest rates, tax rates, public finance, the volume of foreign debts and foreign exchange rates. Among them, methods of finance become the most important control lever. Deepening reform of financial system is the key to keeping on the present track of steady development in the national economy, preventing the possibility of over-heated economic growth, fulfilling the goal put forward by Comrade Deng Xiaoping of attaining a new step forward every several years.

The State Council recently clarified the goals of reform of the financial system: to establish a financial organization system which separates policy finance from commercial finance, lets state commercial banks for the main body and allows the existence of different kinds of financial institutions; to establish the financial market system of unified opening to the outside world, orderly competition and strict control. Therefore, we should seize the opportunity and boldly promote reform of the financial system.

1. Review and Appraisal of China's Financial Reform

During the financial reform in the past decade or so, China's financial system and its operating mechanism witnessed some fundamental changes. Among them, the multiplying forms of financial institutions, the innovation of financial tools and the growth of financial market in particular have transformed more savings into investment and provided many enterprises with external financing. This helped realize a large number of investment and profit-making opportunities and promoted economic growth and income rises. It is indisputable that Chinese financial institutions have experienced remarkable changes. As far as the function of the financial system in promoting the allocation of social resources is concerned, China's financial reform has just begun. Reform in the 1990s is as essential as it is more complex and more difficult. .

Different kinds of financial institutions have come into being along with the establishment of the central bank. The People's Bank of China exclusively assumed the functions of the central bank in 1984, thereby marking the start of diversification in Chinese financial institutions. Toward the end of 1991, Chinese financial institutions included the central bank, the five state banks (Industrial and Commercial Bank of China, Agricultural Bank of China, Bank of China, People's Construction Bank of China, and Bank of Communications) and their branches in different places, four regional commercial banks, 377 financial trust and investment companies, 66 securities companies, 19 finance companies, nine financial leasing companies, 58,200 rural credit cooperatives and 3,421 urban credit cooperatives. During this period China generally moved from the old system of unified bank organizations to the existence of diversified financial institutions.

Initial establishment of the financial market has led to a regional inter-bank borrowing market in China, and the amount of inter-bank loans in the nation had reached 200 billion yuan by 1991. But the money market is not very normal. First, the borrowing is over a long period. The financial institutions do not borrow for regulating the money on hand or for making up their legal reserves, instead they borrow for issuing loans. This gives rise to the following phenomena; on one hand, the excessive savings of the specialized banks in the central bank amounted to 12.6 percent of the total deposits, and on the other, inter-bank borrowing climbed to 100 billion yuan. Second, a unified national market has not taken shape. The regional differences in annual interest rates for the same period may be as large as one percentage point. Third, the benchmark interest rate of the central bank has no power to regulate the borrowing market.

A breakthrough in the past reform is the formation of the Chinese capital market, especially the formation of the securities market. By the end of 1991, the value of securities issued in China totaled 377 billion yuan and their transactions on the market reached 65 billion yuan. The Shanghai and Shenzhen Securities Exchanges started business one after another and the trial stock market made tremendous progress. By the end of June 1992, 40 stocks with a market value of over 60 billion yuan were listed on the two securities exchanges and more than one million people directly invested in stocks. However, the development of Chinese securities market is artificially limited to a considerable extent and has many problems to be solved. The major problems are: the insufficient varieties and small amount of securities and their irrational structure cannot meet public demand; the small and scattered agencies dealing with securities offer inadequate business services; the unsound system of redeeming bonds and guaranteeing their issues affect the credit of bonds; the system of rating bonds has not been established; the interest rates of different bonds are somewhat irrational, all being basically close to the upper limit of state stipulated interest rates, and it is difficult to differentiate the risks involved because the interest rates do not conform to the credit standing of the bond-issuing organizations; the methods of quoting, transaction, delivery and clearance of securities exchange are relatively backward, information is not up-to-date and the unified national market has not been established; the development of the primary market and secondary market is not coordinated and the latter's development falls behind; the management system of the securities market is still imperfect and the laws and regulations governing securities market are inadequate.

Slowness and shortcomings of reform progress have been evidenced in previous financial reform in China, which was a gradual process starting from the above in a planned way and therefore had always been under government control. Clearly, its progress was slow and inadequate and leant toward the old system. The reasons were the restrictions imposed by the political system and ideologies—especially the worry of whether the reform was capitalist or socialist, the over-emphasis of Chinese characteristics and the negation of successful and advanced Western experiences and international practices; there appeared disputes and reversals in reforming the securities market. Restricted by the lack of deep reform in enterprise, such as the lack of clearly defined property rights of enterprises and an unsound system of internal checking and balancing, the claims and obligations of credit loans could not be fully guaranteed and the bank could proceed with other aspects of its business reforms. Influenced by the guiding idea of macro-policies and restricted by the systems of planning, pricing, investment and public finance, some measures of financial reform could not be put into effect. However, for the purpose of promoting the next step of financial reform, it is beneficial to point out the insufficient efforts in the previous reform.

First, deviation from the guiding idea of the central bank. With the general background of reform toward using the market, an important task of the central bank lies in perfecting the financial market mechanism and the bank should not freely enlarge its power and scope of intervening in the activities of social credit on the pretext of the underdeveloped market. In the 1988-1990 period, the central bank laid enormous stress upon the control of social financial activities by the credit plan, thus preventing to a certain extent the growth of financial market mechanism, especially weakening the main role of specialized banks and other financial institutions in the market. This caused the deviation of social credit from the law of value and produced such strange and distorted credit as issuing loans to lesser institutions with conditions attached, appointed loans and special purpose loans.

Second, China's various kinds of financial institutions have not rid themselves of the status of being completely attached to the government. A major factor is the appointment of officials under the present personnel system. Thus, the administrative intervention of banks and other financial institutions by the government at different levels, the department in charge and the central bank is justified because of their official positions. This affects the macro-efficiency of capital. Under such a system, the officials play the leading role and "political risks" always exist in the credit activities. To avoid "political risks," the leaders of some financial institutions prefer the increase of economic risks instead.

Third, the financial monopoly has been further reinforced instead of being broken. Therefore, the environment of normal competition has never been created and the efficiency of the financial industry fell.

Fourth, the very insufficient deepening of the financial market, regional blockades, the lack of financial tools and the sluggish development of the securities market caused the financial market to lag behind the commodity market. This affects to a certain extent the future growth of the Chinese commodity economy.

Fifth, the interest rate reform based on market economy remained untouched on the whole. On the contrary, the planned control of interest rate was strengthened tremendously. In the previous stage of reform, the interest rate's function of being the price of capital and allocating resources was suppressed to a certain extent and not demonstrated.

Sixth, the independence of the central bank in monetary policy was not established, a result influenced by the political system.

Seventh, the system of using notes in credit clearance was suspended mid-way through. Intervened by the chain debts in 1989, reform of clearance that had been decided was mistakenly abolished. The method of entrusting the bank to make collections which embodied the planned commodity economy was forcibly restored. A later reform has to be carried out again.

Eighth, the prolonged use of some short-term emergency measures meant the restoration of the old system. For example, the continued adoption of the Regulations on Cash Management retards the normal progress of commodity transactions. In the management of wage funds, the bank depends on the basic wage fund approved by the labour department to issue cash wages to enterprises and this method is still in force. The control of the amount of loans issued by the urban and rural credit cooperatives seems to remain in place for a long time. All such measures should be abolished in the next stage of reform.

Ninth, the financial supervision has always been exercised mainly by adminstrative orders and documents issued by the central bank and is not restrained by law. The supervision has not been gradually placed on the legal track. This forms a big hindrance to Chinese financial reform in the 1990s.

Tenth, the reform in the insurance industry has always been a weak link, and it was neglected in the previous reform. Contradictions are outstanding, but their solution takes time.

2. Sharp Contradictions Between Lagging Financial Reform and Market Economy

Judged by financial reform as a whole and the historical process of reform, the Chinese financial industry is still in the infant stage in terms. Many deeply hidden contradictions in the reform are gradually being exposed. The fact that the financial system reform falls behind the economic system reform means it cannot meet the needs for the development of market economy. The following are the outstanding contradictions which call for earnest study and swift solutions.

(1) Replacing reform with improvements does not touch the central issues.

As some experts have pointed out, although the people's bank began assuming the functions of the central bank in 1984, it has never enjoyed the legal guarantee of independently making and implementing a monetary policy. At the same time, it also performs some functions of specialized banks, issueing the special-purpose loans and retaining a portion of its profits. The Chinese central bank is a strange institution compared with the central banks in developed countries. The reform of specialized banks has different interpretations in recent years—to let them become enterprises, to emphasize their role as policy banks or to introduce enterprise management. These puzzle the public. Talk of turning them into enterprises has lasted for years. Up to now, none of the banks has become a real enterprise. Actually they follow the system of "eating from the same big bowl" and the reform does not touch the central issues.

(2) Weak macro-control and the increasing pressure from inflation.

Some experts hold that China has used finance as an effective method of economic control in recent years, particularly in the three years of rectification and consolidation. The state adopted a policy of austerity, limiting the scale of loans and controlling the amount of credit by strict planned targets. These measures produced some beneficial effects. Owing to the plan based on the actual figure of the previous year, however, every place tried various means to add supplementary requirements or to surpass the limits in the current year so as to raise its target in the next year. At the same time, the vertical distribution of the credit scale and the horizontal allocation of credit capital are often disconnected; the enlarged scale needs more capital while the enlarged capital needs a bigger scale. The plan decided at the start of the year is often changed in the middle of the year and surpassed at the end of the year. The central bank has to make passive readjustments. These contradictions become sharper with the accelerated development of the national economy. In such places where the targets are insufficient, they manage to produce hidden targets beyond the plan. From the reports every place basically has controlled the scale of loans within the plan. The truth is distorted by false reports, altered items and all tricks possible. In such circumstances the central bank, that is, the people's bank, clearly has insufficient power for macro-control and very limited economic means and administrative measures.

(3) Lack of smooth capital flow and seriously lowered quality of credit assets.

The amount of credit in China totals RMB 2,000 billion

yuan. The continuous flow of such a huge amount in economy should produce remarkable results. However, according to the estimates of authoritative departments, 70 percent of the bank's credit is used for the lowest requirements of enterprise working capital, 15 percent is actually bad debt and only 15 percent may be used by the bank. In some places one-third of the credit become stagnant and one-third is lost to bad debt. In the worst places these loans cannot be repaid. This situation seriously weakens the real function of credit capital and enormously reduces the efficiency and earnings of capital flow. As more than one half of China's credit capital comes from savings deposits, its operating risks increase further. The low quality of credit assets and their large amount, slow turnover and low earnings become so serious that changes have to be introduced.

(4) Confused financial order and seriously disordered competition.

Owing to the lack of financial laws and regulations, the mechanism of self-control and unified strong leadership in recent years, confused financial disorder is fairly striking. Despite repeated prohibitions, there exist the following phenomena: the free raising of interest rates on deposits, setting up financial institutions without approval, exceeding the scale of loans, making changes for convenience, contracting false entrustments and making false inter-bank borrowing. In order to increase their strength and obtain capital, clients or areas of operation, the specialized banks blindly compete among themselves. Some set hindrances against others, delay the delivery of bills and even apply pressure on the enterprises which need to open accounts. Some relax their management and supervision. The original relations between banks and enterprises have become distorted. These not only influence the prestige of banks but also adversely affect the entire financial function and the normal operation of enterprises.

(5) "Caged finance" replaces autonomous finance and deprives finance of its subjective initiative and creativeness.

Some experts are of the opinion that China imposes many restraints on finance—restraints on the scale of credit, on operations, on interest rates and on competition. The long-established monopoly of state banks makes them live in the arms of the state, and they neither run risks nor face any life-and-death competition. The administrative financial system of supplying type makes the issue of credit highly compulsory and denies the financial regulating function through the market. The bank invests most of the money borrowed at a high interest rate in losing enterprises and even in enterprises with more liabilities than assets.

Therefore, the reform of the financial system must be oriented to the market, that is, according to the theory of socialist market economy, to reform the existing financial system and build gradually the financial system and operating mechanism suited to the Chinese conditions.

3. Comparison and Analysis of Programs of Financial System Reform in the 1990s

To meet the needs for developing the socialist market economy, it is generally agreed that the present financial system must be further reformed. However, there are different views on how to conduct reform. The following are the three major representative programs of reform put forward by experts.

(1) The financial system reform in China should be built on the basis of the economic system reform. Only after the establishment of the effective and perfect market economy can the methods and measures of financial reform be carried out. Independent financial system reform is difficult to make effective. Therefore, financial reform should proceed in a planned way. The central bank and the government should gradually form an independent and cooperative relationship. Under the conditions of not giving up such direct macro-control methods as the credit plan, the cash plan and interest rate control, the orientation is a gradual transformation to mainly indirect control. Within a certain period, it is necessary to adopt the method of issuing loans which fixed direction, gradually reduce the scope of policy oriented loans, and give the bank some autonomy in issuing loans. At the same time, such measures of public finance as the interest subsidy and creating funds should be reinforced. As to the financial market,

the main contents of capital market should be bonds in a considerable period in the future. The form of capital financing by issuing stocks should be gradually promoted on a trial basis, but only the stocks of the enterprises which have been transformed according to the regulations of shareholding can be listed on the stock exchanges. The financial system should include mainly specialized banks with a minor section of other business transactions.

(2) Financial reform shall take the lead in China's entire economic reform. According to this program, the composition of savings has undergone big changes since the adoption of the reform and opening policies. The savings of government and enterprises have relatively declined whilst those of the citizens have increased rapidly. This creates the economic basis for developing direct capital financing and shifting the risks of state investment. From an overall view, the advance financial reform may begin with the fostering of the securities market, encouraging enterprises to use capital financing and promoting the transfer and adjustment of enterprise assets. The expectation of finally leading to the reform and innovation of enterprise system may be the best program for deepening economic reform as a whole. The theoretical basis is: By converting the capital into commodities and placing it on the market, the development of a securities market may lessen the pressure on the state banks in their distribution of credit; further reinforcing the function of regulating the market, promoting the rapid formation of key markets and reducing the pressure of inflation; promoting the reform of shareholding system; diffusing the risks of state investment; fostering the financial understanding of the public and solving the general insufficent effort to accumulate enterprises under the dual system, especially the responsibility contract system.

(3) The overall program for financial reform in the 1990s is formulated on the theoretical basis of the socialist market economy and on using successful contemporary Western financial theory and practical experience as reference. The program contains the following main points.

a. The diversified goals of the reform and development of

11

financial institutions and the establishment of independent entities. Because of the absence of clearly defined property rights in the organization system of our financial institutions, China's present financial system with specialized banks as the main body becomes the basic constraint of further reform. The future financial organization system should be based on completely independent property rights and geared to the development of socialist market economy. It should consist of a group of financial institutions of different scales and various forms.

b. The model of capital financing should be transformed into the one that relies mainly on securing residents interest and the use of market. The state will mainly ensure the financing and use of capital for such basic industries as energy, communications and raw materials, and the infrastructrual facilities. The capital needed by the processing and general industries will be mainly solved by the market. Thus, it is necessary to develop a bond market, steadily promote the stock market on a trial basis and set up various investment funds.

c. To give up the credit plan and abolish completely control over the scale of loans in particular. Planned control over direct financing (the amount of bonds and stocks issued) should be replaced by the monetary policy that uses the increase margin of money supply as the medium index. To restore fully the autonomy of issuing loans by all kinds of banks and financial institutions, to separate policy business from commercial business, to reform the central bank's management of loans and to introduce the open market operation at the proper time.

d. The interest rate should be decided by the market. The specific steps are: To abolish the interest rate limit on direct capital financing (mainly that of various bonds) and let the bond issuing organizations decide the interest rate. The central bank will set the benchmark interest rate, thereby forming the real interest rate for borrowing.

The first program is a conservative one. It emphasizes the gradual replacement of the old system along with the improved external environment brought by the financial system reform. But the stagnant financial reform in the past decade or so is precisely the result of such thinking. The financial system reform needs some necessary external conditions, but there exist mutually related relations between the financial system and the economic system. While the financial system waits for the economic system reform to blaze its way, certain aspects of financial system restrict the smooth advance of economic system reform. Under the condition of retarded financial reform in China, the adoption of this program will block the advance of financial system reform and even the formation of the mechanism of market economy.

The second program takes the accelerated fostering of securities market as the key to financial reform and expects that this fostering will promote the economic system reform. This program at least neglects the two following facts. First, the development of a securities market is founded on the development of a shareholding system. Under the condition of unclear property rights of enterprises, blind development of a securities market before reform of the shareholding system is like building a castle in the air. Secondly, the securities market, that is, the channel of direct capital financing for enterprises, is based on the indirect capital financing system and other component elements of the financial market. This market cannot develop in advance.

The development of a securities market is inseparable from the different kind of financial institutions that are active on the market as middle men, investors or capital financiers. Therefore, the absence of a sound organization system of financial institutions makes the development of a securities market rootless. This development will certainly be restricted without the various kinds of investment funds and the guarantee of enterprise bonds by the banks. Moreover, judged by the history of financial market development, indirect finance is the basis of direct finance. The main reason why enterprises can and will issue bonds is the cost of bonds is lower than bank loans, but the scale of the bond issuing enterprises must be large, their prestige high and their issued sum large. As only a small number of enterprises meet these conditions, the vast majority of them depend on bank loans for their capital needs.

As a matter of fact, even in some developed countries such

as Japan, direct financing only developed in the 1970s and 1980s. The proportion of direct financing in the total financing is 18.3 percent in Japan, 59.3 percent in the United States and 19.8 percent in Germany.

Therefore, the second program does not have the support of correct theory and is impracticable.

The third program puts forward detailed goals and the model for establishing a financial system suited to the socialist market economy. However, it has two weak points. First, it fails to talk about how the bank shall carry out enterprise management. This is precisely the difficult problem that the reform of financial system cannot go around and must tackle, and it is also the basis of financial system reform as a whole. Without the enterprise management of banks, the setting of interest rates by the market will only cause confusion on the financial market, and the abolishment of control over the scale of loans will cause the uncontrolled scale of credit loans. Second, the program does not touch on the steps, road and breakthrough of the reform.

From the comparison and analysis of the above three representative programs of financial system reform, we may raise the following points: First, as financial system reform in China falls behind its economic system reform, the former calls for bigger efforts and cannot wait until the economic system reform creates a better environment for the financial reform. Therefore, the designing of any program should pay attention to the synchronization and connection with the economic system reform. Secondly, financial reform cannot be separated from the objective law of development of a financial system, and the designing of a program needs the support of scientific economic theory. Thirdly, the reform of banks along the enterprise line must be fully emphasized in the program. If the enterprise operations of banks remains unsolved, other financial reform measures cannot produce the expected results. Fourth, the merits of the program of financial system reform are mainly expressed in its rational steps and methods.

4. Main Aspects of China's Financial Reform

1) Central Bank

(1) The macro-control over the financial market by the central bank must be reinforced. As the state's highest organ of financial policy decision and financial management, the central bank must exercise macro-management, organization and coordination of the financial market and lead it to normal operation.

The central bank is essentially the bank of issuing currency, the bank of banks and the bank exercising macro-control. Therefore, it shall use its special position and advantages to play the invested role, that is, to watch the two "sluice gates" in macro-control—the amount of issued currency and the total scale of credit. However, in practice our central bank has failed to take good care of the two "sluice gates." In 1992, for instance, compared with 1991, bank loans went up 19.6 percent and cash supply rose 36.4 percent or 19 percentage points higher than the sum of economic and price rises. It may be said that both the amounts of currency issued and currency supplied were out of control. This caused a deficit of 23 billion yuan in public finance. In fact, the real deficit should be 80 billion yuan after internal and foreign borrowing are deducted from the revenue according to the Western method of calculation. If this situation were to continue, the future would be unimaginable.

It is necessary under the present conditions to strengthen the macro-control of the central bank by all means and strive to turn the situation in the beneficial direction. At the same time, we shall make the greatest effort to reform the traditional system of the central bank. The defects of China's central bank formed under the traditional system are especially outstanding in the following aspects. It may be the world's top central bank in terms of the size of organization, large numbers of staff, wide business scope and management disorder. The U.S. Federal Reserve Bank has altogether 12 regional branches, 25 sub-branches and 2,000 staff members. The People's Bank of China has 2,400 branches and sub-branches and 160,000 staff members. The basic function of a central bank should be the macro-control of finance and banking, but the Chinese central bank even handles gold and jewellery. Unless the bank can thoroughly transform its function in the future, it will not be able to undertake the important task of macro-control.

(2) Why does the central bank need its independent position? According to one opinion, the basic reason for its independence is that the monetary policy must be ensured by the system. Since what the statesmen and government leadership are interested in while taking an action often goes against the sustained protection of anti-inflation policy, establishing a system to entrust a monetary authority, which is independent of the government, to formulate and implement the monetary policy is the best way to guarantee the discipline of monetary policy.

The second opinion holds that the central bank should be independent but that independence may be under government leadership. At the same time, the central bank should coordinate and cooperate with the government and support the latter's economic policy under the precondition of stabilizing the currency. The chief task of the governor of central bank is to guard against the increase of money supply and not agree to the government's attempt to raise freely the amount of money. The central bank should cooperate with the government but the cooperation must have a limit, that is, the stabilization of currency. For example, if the government wants the central bank to buy government bonds, this cannot be accepted because it is equal to asking the central bank to issue more banknotes. The central bank should maintain independent operation but the operation should be kept within the government. The goals of the central bank and the government are not the same—the former aims at maintaining currency and price stabilization while the latter aims at economic growth and political ends. Therefore, they should coordinate well and their good coordination will benefit the state enormously. It will be a great loss for the state if the government does not accept the proposals of the central bank.

Experts of the World Bank briefed the relationship between the central bank and the government in Malaysia. Its central bank is independent but not independent from the government. If the government and the central bank hold different views, the latter may appeal to the parliament. However, the appeal never takes place because they keep good coordination. They have a coordination committee attended by the secretary general of the Ministry of Finance on behalf of the government. Different opinions and demands can be settled in the committee which meets twice a year. Afterward the central bank is responsible for carrying out the monetary policy.

According to the third opinion, the independence of the central bank should be in essence rather than in form. The Japanese central bank is relatively independent. The Law of Bank of Japan (that is the Law of Central Bank) stipulates that the Ministry of Finance representing the government exercises wide supervision over the bank. Legally the bank is not independent but actually the important monetary policies such as the discount rate are decided by the bank itself. Although the bank needs to coordinate with the government, the final decision is made by the bank. Therefore, independence should be judged by essence and not by form and law. Judged by form and law, the Bank of England (a consolidated central bank) has the least independence among the banks of the developed countries.

However, it habitually opposes the too many interventions of the central bank by the government and actually enjoys great independence.

(3) The independence of a central bank lies in the reliability of ensuring the monetary policy. What is the goal of monetary policy? Some experts say that the main goal of monetary policy should be stabilized currency. The policy of stabilized currency can fully support economic growth because a stabilized economic environment is beneficial to absorbing investment and savings. Some people are of the opinion that inflation may produce compulsory savings and the use of savings in investment will promote economic growth. A number of Latin American countries precisely took this road of undertaking construction by means of "inflation". What was the outcome? It may be proved by a comparison between Venezuela and Taiwan. When the

per-capita income was US$ 100 in Taiwan, the income in Venezuela reached US$ 500. Taiwan took the road of stabilized development while Venezuela took the road of development by inflation. The results were: the per-capita income reached US$ 7,000-8,000 in Taiwan and it was only US$ 1,000-2,000 in Venezuela. This offers a painful lesson.

If the monetary policy of central bank is not stabilizing the currency, this will certainly result in alternating tight and loose policy, thus leading economic development up and down. A stabilized monetary policy needs not to be tightened. Generally the cause of alternating tight and loose monetary policy is that the central bank first carries out inflationary policy beyond its limit and then eagerly wants to shift to the tight policy. The outcome of alternating too tight and too loose policy is extremely harmful to the economy.

Some experts pointed out that the monetary policy of the Republic of South Korea was dependent on the government policy of economic development in the 1960s and 1970s. Therefore, the monetary policy was expansionary during this period. The succeeding government in the 1980s adopted the tight monetary policy of stabilizing prices, which reduced the inflation rate from 20 percent to 5 percent. Its monetary policy in the 1960s and 1970s was somewhat similar to that of China in the mid-1980s, but the former's micro-basis is different from that of China. In the Republic of South Korea the micro-mechanism is one of self-restraint; when the enterprises want expansion, they also assume investment risks. The present Chinese enterprises, however, lack the mechanism of self-restraint. Therefore, the expansionary monetary policy would have more serious consequences in China.

The monetary policy is basically a policy of restraint. It aims at checking or restricting the acquisition of capital so that with maintained price stability and economic balance as a whole, the society may keep a balance beween the amount of absorbed capital and needed capital. Hence the following contradiction. To maintain price stability, the money authority should strive to limit the amount of required capital, and to promote economic growth, it is also the supplier of capital. Can the monetary policy of central bank fulfil these functions at the same time? Certainly not. Therefore, the monetary policy should have the single goal of stabilizing price.

The wide or narrow goal of monetary policy is closely related to the independence of central bank. If the goal of the monetary policy is single and clear, that is, price stability, the central bank will have clearly defined responsibilities and obligations and more independence. If the goal of monetary policy is very wide, the central bank is not much different from other government departments. The government will continuously put forward changing demands on the central bank within the very wide goal, and the latter will enjoy little independence. Thus, the single and clear goal of monetary policy is complementary to the independence of the central bank and is also necessary for ensuring currency and economic stability.

Experts also pointed out at the same time that monetary policy should be coordinated with the other economic policies of the government and supported with the goal of ensuring price stability. The monetary policy should also be coordinated with other policies, especially financial policy. The budgetary balance of such countries and regions as Japan, Singapore and Taiwan is a very important reason to ensure their low inflation.

(4) Some experts suggest the need for establishing supervising agencies for the monetary policy in order to implement it effectively. The supervising agency of the New Zealand government asks the president of the central bank to fulfil his announced goals during his tenure. He shall submit a bi-annual statement of policy to the prime minister and an annual report on policy implementation to the parliament. An outside organization appointed by the prime minister will evaluate the work of the president of the central bank. Of course, the supervision of monetary policy can also be completed by publishing the targets of the total money supply. The system of supervising monetary policy is not only to assure the public and keep the state clear, but also to maintain the vigor of the central bank to fulfil its announced goals.

Foreign experts also made a deep analysis of China's monetary policy. Macro-economic instability and imbalance appeared in China in the latter half of the 1980s and one of the major factors was the absence of an efficient monetary policy. The monetary policy was not strict and even gave strong support to and provided connivance for over-investment, over-heated economy and inflation pressure. The policy reaction and revision were often slow, and sometimes wavered between two extremes in a brief period. All this led to violent fluctuations in the economy. The monetary policy failed to control the economic problems in advance and only dealt with them passively later.

Chinese monetary policy bears pressure from many sources: First, pressure from the system. Non-centralized reform leads to huge investment expansion in various departments, places and enterprises and the reform has not solved budgetary restrictions. The needs for capital are great and eager in the beginning. Secondly, China has embarked an ambitious plan of development which requires enormous investment. Thirdly, the Chinese state-owned enterprises are both production organizations and "micro-societies," and any monetary policy of checking the enterprise production and investment activities naturally leads to unacceptable social consequences. Fourth, the defects of the public finance system have to be remedied by the financial system. The above features explain the special urgency of aquiring a monetary policy of restraint in China and the tremendous difficulties of its implementation. These features also indicate that China must adopt such a policy in order to maintain economic stability.

Inadequate independence of China's central bank has become a major restraint of the system in effectively formulating and carrying out the monetary policy. The macro-economic instability in the latter half of the 1980s should be attributed in a large degree to the high growth policy. If the then central bank had enjoyed more independence, it could have exercised greater restraint over a government that deviated from its announced policy of stable growth. An independent central bank is very important in China in order to resist the loan requests by the ministries, local governments and state-owned enterprises.

The independence of central bank may be within the government, that is, the independence of carrying out the monetary policy. To solve the potential conflicts between the monetary policy and other fields of the government's wide economic plans it is necessary to establish a close consultation system between the central bank and the government. The consultations shall follow the guideline that as long as the central bank keeps its publicized goal of stabilizing prices, it should support the economic policy of government.

(5) As suggested by World Bank experts, China needs the creation of a monetary commission or a central bank commission to ensure the independence of the central bank and coordinate with the other economic policies. This standing commission will collect opinions and suggestions from all possible sources and comprise a small group of economic and technical experts. Within the power permitted by the State Council, it may make quick decisions on key economic variables such as the interest rate and instruments of credit.

To maintain price and economic stability, China shall have a strong central bank. But its credit standing, dignity, real strength and independence depend on its management level. Only when it displays its real ability in formulating and implementing monetary policy can it win the support and confidence of the public and receive power from the government.

According to the opinion of World Bank experts, to raise the professional level of central bank at the present time, it is important that the central bank expands the extent of data collection and statistical analysis, and raises quality, effectiveness and its research and analytic ability. Experiences in Japan, the Republic of South Korea and other countries all showed that a strong research department may present the central bank with valuable and timely suggestions on the trends of economic development and that remarkable research results, to a large extent, depend on training and having high-quality researchers.

Experts also suggested that in view of the possible money expansion triggered by local influence, the central bank may set up five or six regional branches in different economic areas which should be managed by their presidents directly appointed by the central bank. By breaking up provincial boundaries this will reduce the intervention in the monetary policy by local governments to the lowest limit. At the same time, this may also help the integration of local banking and shatter regional division.

2) Instruments of Monetary Policy

What instruments of monetary policy should be selected? Experts hold that the differences in the independence of the central bank in various countries are often expressed in the number and features of the instruments of monetary control available to the central bank. The selection of these instruments in developing countries meets many restraints. Because of the absense of good capital and money markets, these countries tend to adopt crude, direct and adminsitrative means of monetary control. The more the central bank depends on this method, the more it cannot actively and flexibly regulate finance. When the central bank is relatively weak, it will depend on direct control to implement the policy. But the main dependence of this method also carries many drawbacks. First, the setting of a ceiling on loans limits the absorption of deposits and reduces the desire to save, thereby lowering the effects of monetary control. Secondly, direct control of credit often combines with the administrative allocation of credit. This causes the allocation of resources by bureaucratic bodies and dogmatically decided political standards in the policy of credit, thus ignoring the quality of the asset structure of the bank, and the increase of bad debt. Thirdly, the ceiling of credit may entice uncontrolled financial media and financial instruments to compete with or undermine controlled institutions. By encroaching on the control of credit, this may finally weaken monetary control. Fourth, direct control is not beneficial to developing an effective method of resources allocation such as money and capital markets.

As to the relations between direct control and indirect control, experts hold that under the present conditions China cannot completely avoid direct control, but must transform it gradually into indirect control as the main method. At the same time, many policies, including the use of securities, may be adopted.

Some experts believe that in the early period of development of many countries, they often adopt direct control of credit and the speed of changing from direct to indirect control differs according to their conditions. In the case of China, it is better to quicken this change. However, China cannot entirely depend on the control through interest rates and still needs quantity control. Quantity control may also be an indirect one, for instance, the control of the basic money of the central bank.

According to World Bank experts, a market-oriented economy should depend more on indirect means to realize stability because indirect means are flexible and can reduce policy vacillation. This vacillation is what China has experienced since the mid-1980s. Of course, the control of the total amount of credit may complement the indirect means. But more reliance should be placed on indirect than direct control.

The World Bank suggested that when China adopts indirect control to replace the present control of loan scale, it may choose the following policy instruments. A part of the reserves may be bonds of the People's Bank to form the basis of the bank's fund market and at the same time become collateral for inter-bank market transactions. Open market operations may provide the People's Bank with an important and flexible indirect policy instrument; the People's Bank may undertake rediscount of short-term government bonds and manage or issue short-term treasury bills. A part of the loans extended by the People's Bank to specialized banks may be changed to open market business, that is, changing the short-term loans directly distributed to specialized banks by the People's Bank to bonds.

World Bank experts hold that to stablize the economy, more indirect control means have to be used. The indirect control needs the establishment and integration of the market. Only the regulating of the market can make indirect control effective.

Taiwan scholars profoundly analyzed Taiwan's experience of gaining stable development by regulating the interest rate. In the early 1950s, the fiscal and financial situation was very bad. In order to stimulate investment, the authorities artificially reduced the interest rate to a very low level. As a result, savings did not flow into the banks and the authorities had to depend on inflation. Experts suggested changing this situation by using the regulating function of interest rates, that is, making the interest rate higher than the inflation rate. The then Taiwan authorities adopted this suggestion by raising the annual interest rate to 127 percent when the inflation rate was 120 percent. Afterward huge amounts of savings flowed into the banks, which provided the authorities with construction funds and restricted inflation. Therefore, the effective use of interest rates may solve the contradiction between monetary stability and the promotion of economic development. The interest rate went down with the decline of the price index. The then economists suggested the adoption of value ensured interest rates for savings deposits, but this suggestion was not accepted. When the interest rate decreased with the decline of the price index, this aroused many complaints from the public. If the suggestion were accepted, this problem would not have appeared. It is correct for the mainland to adopt value ensured savings deposits.

3) Oriented Loans

According to experts, the issuing of Oriented loans (policy loans) is not a good method but it has to be adopted in certain periods. Therefore, it is necessary to study earnestly the scope of policy-oriented loans, the management by separate accounts (policy-oriented loans and operating loans) or the establishment of a specialized organization, and the strengthening of such financial measures as interest subsidy and creation of funds. The bank should be given some independence in issuing policy-oriented loans.

Experts from Oxford University hold that when the market is imperfect, it is still necessary to choose a limited amount of oriented loans. The loans issued by the World Bank and the International Monetary Fund to developing countries for promoting structural adjustments belong to oriented loans. These loans are needed at present in China. Its regional imbalance calls for this kind of loans to support regional policy and this need cannot entirely depend on the market. However, oriented loans incur such costs as political intervention and corruption. The problems in China's oriented loans direction are: Firstly, the too large scale. Secondly, the goal of these loans is questionable. For example, loans are used to support enterprises suffering losses which is harmful to structural adjustments. To do a good job in handling these loans, experts suggested: a. Policy-oriented loans should be separated from commercial loans and a development bank may be established to deal with policy-oriented loans. b. Local governments should be allowed to issue bonds in support of their infrastructure so as to shoulder part of policy-oriented loans. c. The government only asks the bank to give preference to some industries of prior development, but does not directly distribute loans by instructions. Specific loans should be appraised and handled by the bank independently.

World Bank delegates pointed out that some people oppose oriented loans because they may be used to support enterprises sustaining losses or distort the rational distribution of resources and lead to corruption when the distribution of such loans is at the will of government. But it is inevitable to use this kind of loan for supporting the growth of key trades in China. But it should be pointed out that there is the danger of mistaken resources allocation by such loans. For this purpose, the use of oriented loans should follow the following principles: Firstly, to choose the smallest possible number of supported key trades. Secondly, the government only provides the bank with the principle of enjoying prior loans and should let the bank decide the specific loan receiving organizations on the basis of its own appraisal. Thirdly, loans should be handled by accounts separated from those of other assets, and the work of issuing loans may be gradually transferred to a special financial institution. Fourth, with the maturity of the market, these loans will be reduced step by step and finally eliminated.

Taiwan experts are of the opinion that the discussion on the oriented loans is essentially a choice of distributing resources by market or by mandatory planning. The former method needs the careful use of a small amount of these loans as a supplement, if these loans are used everywhere, it will lead to low efficiency and corruption. Having compared the development of China with that of the "four small dragons" (South Korea, Taiwan, Hong Kong and Singapore), some experts concluded that savings in China are not lower than those of the latter, and the gap of development lies in the low investment efficiency in China. The Chinese investment efficiency (the amount of investment divided by the newly increased part in national income) is only 15-20 percent, lower than that of India, and the investment efficiency stands at 40-50 percent in Japan and the "four small dragons." The gap in development originates from investment efficiency. So the Chinese government needs to consider the question of using the market or mandatory planning to allocate resources.

4) Supervision of Banking System

World Bank experts say that it needs a supervision and control environment to implement monetary policy successfully and protect the healthy operation of financial institutions. In the last two years, the banking system suffered from deterioration of assets which has to be prevented to ensure effective economic recovery. This is a deep-rooted question of the system and can be lessened and finally solved only by financial, fiscal and enterprise reform in a comprehensive way.

Specialized banks continue to issue loans to deficit enterprises according to the will of government, this is blood transfusion, but this cannot last long and may lead banks into bankruptcy in the end. A better method is to auction these enterprises in the shareholding form and reorganize their useful parts. Experiences in various countries indicated the need to settle financial assets. The sooner the better.

Although Chinese banks do not have much competition, there are still risks in their operation. The state banks lack serious consideration in issuing loans for they are not answerable to the funds and tend to keep expanding in this business. At the same time, they have the duty to save the state-owned enterprises from sustaining losses. The state-owned enterprises like banks are subject to soft restrictions and dare to borrow loans. In short, these constitute the risks of issuing loans.

The World Bank emphasized: It is necessary to establish a cautious supervision and management system. The People's Bank is displaying its auditing ability but it hardly has any careful management system. It should make its auditing work ensure the conservative operation of financial institutions and control risks in their business. At the same time, the People's Bank should be granted the necessary authority and administrative power to rectify the non-conservative operation of financial institutions. It should also stipulate the reserves for loan losses corresponding to the risks of financial institutions in the composition of their assets, and provide professional training for the thousands of its auditors.

Experts pointed out the need to develop and perfect accounting standards. Chinese accounting standards and system are designed according to the needs of central planned economy and their information system centers on ensuring the unity with central instructions. These systems should be thoroughly revised to provide all the necessary information for deciding conservative management under the market-oriented economy, and to coordinate China's general and departmental accounting standards, and enterprise auditing method with international standards.

The management information system should be developed. Owing to the lack of a sound information system, there is a time gap in the response to Chinese government policy. Up to now, the price index is still fixed by the year and late-coming information creates difficulties for the monetary authorities. For instance, the delayed learning about current situation cannot but adopt extreme policies. The reform of accounting and auditing systems will raise the information value of reports.

The modernized payment and settlement system and sound legal system are of key importance in the financial reform.

5) Capital Market

As to the opportunity for developing the capital market in China today, some experts hold that the key work of financial reform at present in China is perfecting the existing banking system; some others hold that the development of a capital market should not start until the completion of the banking system. Experts of China's State Commission of Economic Restructuring believe that the reform and perfection of existing banking system are one important aspect of reform, but accelerated development of a capital market is also necessary. The reasons are: Firstly, all the present task of financing is imposed on the bank, its pressure and risk are both tremendous because of the short-term savings and long-term loans and the risk may be shared by the development of a capital market. Secondly, the development of a capital market can promote the transformation of the enterprises' mechanism. Different from the banks of Japan and other countries, Chinese banks exercise soft restrictions on enterprises, but relatively hard restriction on enterprises can be realized through financing on the capital market. Thirdly, the increased desire for investment by families calls for more varieties of financial capital to meet their needs.

6) Non-bank Financial Institutions

As to the financial institutions, some experts have pointed out that the non-bank financial institutions in different countries all occupy a very important position in terms of their number and amount of financing, and develop faster than the banks. Owing to the autonomy of non-bank financial institutions in operation and deciding interest rates, they become one kind of substitute for banks and play a major role in economic development. Chinese non-bank financial institutions are gradually being established with the economic development in China. For example, since the banks could not handle trust business, the establishment of a group of trust companies has been approved; since the big banks could not undertake the credit for small enterprises and individually run businesses, some rural credit cooperatives have been established; since the issued securities keep on increasing, securities companies have been established. Some organizations are tried out for reform experiment. In short, experiences in various countries have shown the establishment of financial institutions is decided by two fundamental principles, the economic principle and macro-control principle.

World Bank experts hold: China faces the question of how to manage and develop non-bank financial institutions and how to develop the organization investors. These may become an important aspect of developing the securities business in China. The investors of pension, insurance and trust organizations will play a role in the securities market and they may become bridges between individual investors and the companies with listed securities on the market. In the vast territory of China, if individual persons are allowed to enter the market, it is necessary to let these organization investors play their role. They will provide residents with investment places outside the bank and become important organizers in the capital market, especially in organizing individual investors to enter the market. Therefore, they should receive assistance in the following ways. For instance, they may be allowed to increase their ability through setting up joint ventures, and stipulations will be worked out relating to their entry, withdrawal, accounting and legal affairs.

Some experts believe: The current transfer of assets in China is realized only by savings and loans, too much capital flows through the bank system and especially too many bad debts are shouldered by the bank. All this constitutes a big problem. Its solution needs the establishment of intermediates outside banks to develop another financing channel which can transfer the burden of commercial banks. This is more important in China than in other nations. This financing channel includes mutual-aid funds, insurance, pension funds, trust funds and housing funds.

In the future ten years, the emphasis of China's financial reform should be laid on the establishment of a modernized bank system because during the initial stage of capital accumulation, the bank deposit is an investment of little risk and stable income to the investors and the capital may be invested in useful fields through banks.

The Chinese bank exercises soft restrictions on enterprises and the latter are subject to the soft restrictions of the budget. Therefore, if the bank deposit becomes the only financing channel, the bank's pressure and risk will be larger than those of other countries. So the development of a capital market cannot wait until the completion of bank reform.

Some experts put forward the need for solving the greater economic environment in deepening China's financial reform. Isolated financial reform does not work and any reform must be coordinated with other reforms in different fields, especially in planning, finance and materials systems. It is necessary to reinforce the market system, solve the policy lag, strengthen economic analysis and market feedback, and change the use of old methods to solve all problems. At the same time, legislative work will be reinforced to change gradually from rule by man to rule by law. The reform of the financial system, if included in the shift from direct control to indirect control, will be easily realized.

Chapter II
Prerequisites for Financial Reform

Chinese financial departments have undergone great changes since the 1980s. More than a decade ago, all construction funds for projects were allocated from the treasury. At that time there was no central bank, the financial savings of families were very small and largely involuntary, and the bank was only a cashier working to the instructions of government. Now the financial institutions have multiplied in number and diversified, the savings of residents have exceeded 40 percent of the gross national product, the importance of loans has surpassed that of the construction fund in the government's budget, and the central bank has played an increasingly significant role. Maybe the most convincing fact is that the monetary policy has become the main regulating means of stabilizing and developing the economy. The interest rate played a small role more than ten years ago, and it now stands as one of the most powerful means of indirect policy influencing the general demand by the government.

World Bank experts appraised the functions of financial policy around the four fields: Firstly, the macro-economic stability; secondly, the mobilization of capital; thirdly, the allocation of resources; fourthly, the contribution of financial reform to other reforms (for example, the reform of industrial departments). In every field, Chinese policy makers face rough choices. Because the market-oriented financial reform is not only limited to itself, its contribution to the more extensive goals of economic development and price stability must also be appraised.

1. Macroeconomic Policy and Financial Development

The most important contribution of financial reform is the promotion of economic stability, and unless the reform proceeds in a stabilized macro-economic environment, there will be more instability. Therefore, the reform in financial departments begins with strengthening the existing system and letting the central bank control the money supply effectively. To do this, the authorities concerned need to accelerate the building of the system and legislative reform and adjust the policy in more extensive fields.

1) Actions to Be Adopted by the Government

Experts hold that the government is responsible for macroeconomic stability and overall economic policy. As to the question of money, it is jointly responsible with the People's Bank of China. The bank is in charge of the management of money, and its duty is the maintenance of monetary stability rather than ensuring high-speed economic growth and full employment. The stability of currency is vital to the prospects of Chinese financial development and economic growth, and the success of reform. The conflicts in the special relations between extensive economic goals and monetary policy exist in every country and this is so no matter how much the central bank enjoys autonomy and authority over monetary policy. The argument between the central bank and critics generally originates from the different choice, price stability or economic growth. The government's behaviour has dual meaning here: Framing measures to reinforce the function of indirect monetary policy means, accelerating the system building, using fiscal policy to solve the financial difficulties of central and local governments and the large and medium-sized state-owned enterprises.

(1) Building of Organization System

Some experts believe that since 1985 China has made tremendous progress in monetary management and gained valuable experiences and painful lessons. With regard to China's more complex and more market-oriented economy in the 1990s, the appearence of a new, more specialized and more institutionalized mechanism will be only a matter of time. Strict control of money supply is of vital significance at the crucial moment when the government decides to proceed with the key price reform in big strides.

According to experts, in addition to Chinese economy becoming more complex and decentralized and with the monetary policy intervention increasingly depending on indirect policy instruments, it becomes more necessary and urgent to establish policy decision and supervision organizations such as the monetary committee or the central bank committee. The more the financial authorities depend on indirect policy instruments, the more they need to react quickly (the shortest possible time between information and the feedback of policy decision). As to the People's Bank of China, "going to the market" is its most pressing task. As the primary and secondary money and capital markets grow, policy operation will intervene more in liquidity and cost of capital. The changes of China's economic structure will continue to alter the channel by which monetary policy influences the short-term economic activities. To support the coordinated intervention of the Ministry of Finance and the People's Bank of China, it is necessary to control strictly the total volume of money, renew the system and establish the mechanism of policy feedback.

An important step in system building is the creation of a high-level and non-political policy-decision-making organization which engages in daily management to promote macro-economic stability by properly integrating financial and monetary policies. There should be some overall guiding principles relating to the organization of the committee, its composition and its position in the political system (inside and outside the central bank).

a. It is a standing committee making all possible efforts to ask opinions and suggestions from all fields, and it has a small group of economic and technical experts who may give suggestions but not vote in the final decision.

b. An upper limit should be set to the amount of loans issued to the government by the People's Bank (which should be uncorporated into the Bank Law currently being drafted). The committee should be specially authorized to refuse the supply of loans to the government when the money situation demands so.

c. The committee's form of organization should suit the degree of independence in the operation of monetary policy —something between complete independence (like the central bank committee of the Deutsche Federal Bank) and limited independence (like the central banks in some countries that are restricted by government monetary and economic instructions). The publicly acknowledged link between the independence of the central bank and price stability must be firmly kept in mind. However, the above-mentioned independence can be gradually realized only when the public, other economic organizations and political organizations believe that the new system can be more successful in maintaining domestic price stability. In spite of occasional differences in opinions, the central bank and the ministry of finance may form natural allies with the committee in stabilizing prices and opposing narrow departmental interests. Most central banks need the cooperation of the ministry of finance and other organizations because they cannot operate in a vacuum.

d. The central bank committee should have sufficient power to make quick decisions in matters concerning key economic variables such as interest rate, other short-term money and credit instruments. The committee's power shall be limited to what the State Council permits at the start. The transfer of the right to decide monetary policy from the direct control of central government to the central bank committee will help the gradual non-politicalization and specialization of the monetary policy.

e. No matter what degree of independence the central bank has, the committee must be responsible to the public, which helps get its understanding and support in the painful period of restricted cash now. In short, strength, reputation, dignity and independence will depend on its management level.

(2) Tax System Reform

Any central bank, irrespective of its independence, will face the pressure of government when the fiscal situation becomes bad. If the revenue of central government declines, the business of state-owned enterprises is not good, the fiscal expenditure and subsidy increase and large financial deficits (clear or unclear) appear, the People's Bank of China will face the same pressure. Chinese financial revenue mainly depends on the state-owned enterprises, particularly the monopolist delivery of profit to the government. However, the huge loss of financial revenue and the change in the responsibility system of financial expenditures that accompany the reform have caused large financial deficits and restricted social financial outlays of government and investment in infrastructure. This pressure can only match a comparatively large demand of central government, which does not come out unless within the framework of macro-economic stability where the tax system has been decisively revised and the budgetary expenditure further rationalized. It is now urgent to adopt measures of improving the structure, particularly the measures to enlarge the tax base and accelerate the reform in state-owned enterprises. The structural question is the most important obstacle in the reform of financial departments and continued delay in financial reform will adversely affect the macro-economic stability (such as the provision of money to the financial budget and state-owned enterprises by the People's Bank of China) and the effective allocation of resources (such as direct loans to and financing of the state-owned enterprises which cannot survive).

Judged by maintaining domestic stability and raising micro-economic efficiency, the reform of enterprises tax is the key to fiscal reform. In collecting the income tax from enterprises which borrowed new loans, the repaid part of the principal of loans should not be deducted from the profit. Finally all the reduction and exemption of tax on the principal of loans will be abolished. This reform will improve the government revenue remarkably, and the change from repaying the loan before tax to repaying the loan after tax may restrict investment and promote the more efficient use of capital. This reform will make the Chinese enterprise tax system come closer to the international system.

The expanded right to make decisions by enterprises and local governments enormously reduced the proportion of central government's budgetary revenue in the gross domestic product from 1973 to 1988 (a drop of more than 13 percentage points). This reduction was caused by the huge fall of industrial profit and also caused by the adjustments of major (relative) prices and the sharpened competition among township enterprises. This process brought benefits to the economy, but it also brought serious difficulties to the central budget and the demand for tremendous loans from the public sectors. The shortage of capital for investment in the public sectors was basically made up by relaxing bank and other domestic loans. This expanding credit policy was the most direct reason for the serious inflation in a period in the 1980s. It has become an urgent task to solve the financial difficulties of the central government and state-owned enterprises, but the proposed repayment of loans after tax has been put aside. Positive adoption of this proposal will mark the government's promise of proceeding the tax and enterprise reforms, and of strengthening the use of interest rates as an indirect means of carrying out the monetary policy and as a means of distributing the micro-interests.

2) Function of the People's Bank: Systems Building

The People's Bank of China ceased to be a commercial bank in 1984. From that time on, it has made enormous progress in the process of building itself into the Chinese central bank and the supervisor of financial departments. In spite of these achievements, many experts emphasized that the building of systems is still an inevitable prerequisite for further improving the formulation and implementation of the monetary policy and deepening the financial reform.

(1) Carrying Out Anti-inflation Monetary and Credit Policies

Experts are of the opinion that in the countries where the central bank has wide powers over the monetary policy, the anti-inflation goal in money supply growth is generally strictly observed and earnestly ensured. When there is the threat of uncontrolled inflation in China, successful tight monetary policy will immediately follow. The rapid expansion of credit and its role along the cycle may be explained by the two points below.

a. During the economic cycle, the inherent stabilizing role of finance is weak, which is expressed by the very low structural elasticity in the increase of revenue. In the stage of economic recession, the adoption of the expanding financial policy by the central government to stimulate economy is seriously restricted. In the stage of economic growth, the company tax (unchanged by contract for many years) and personal income tax (the amount is insignificant) cannot control the excessive total demand. Therefore, the government has to depend on domestic loans in a recession and on administrative control during economic growth (particularly the control of investment).

b. Under the condition of soft budget restriction and lower repayment costs of loans after tax, severe administrative control is more effective than indirect means to limit the excessive demand for credit.

Allowing enterprises and local government-made policy decisions means decentralized demand and reduces the regulating role of planning. On the other hand, the use of indirect policy means does not make the factors of price, budget and profit exercise effective restrictions on those who make economic policies. To maintain macro-economic stability, a major problem in managing credit is the process of fomulating an annual credit plan. The financing needs of the public sector must be considered so that the non-inflationary credit plan faces a choice between expanding loans to the government and reducing loans to other economic departments. The regulating role of macro-economic monetary policy is weekened by this negotiation process from below, and the policy lays stress on the demand for credit (fixed assets and working capital credit) for final borrowers. Once the credit needs of departments and regions increase, the People's Bank of China (head office) is hardly able to resist the pressure of enlarging the plan and this enlarged plan is perhaps completely contrary to macro-economic stability and the international balance of payments. In a year without crisis, a credit plan containing an increase of a small amount may be approved earlier in the year, but it is an impracticable plan and very difficult to carry out. During the whole year loans will be continuously added to the plan.

The process of formulating the credit plan should be reversed by starting from the above. The reasonable scale of credit expansion should be decided at the very beginning and the plan should include the demand of designated loans by the government. The central bank committee should play the main role in working out the anti-inflationary monetary and credit policies. In view of this, the People's Bank of China should raise its technical ability and acquire the necessary political support so as to implement the adopted plan. In carrying out the strategy of anti-inflationary economic growth, the steadiness and continuity of policy are very important in maintaining reputation and further influencing the expectation. Besides, the People's Bank of China should detach itself from the process of distributing credit and this work will be specifically done by other organizations within prescribed scale.

Another area that needs reform is in the loans extended to the specialized banks, the direct loans to enterprises and regions and departments by the People's Bank. In the annual credit plan the specialized banks may receive loans from the People's Bank equivalent to about one-third of their capital; the loans bear an interest rate lower than the market one and can be used repeatedly on a permanent basis and with continued increases of their amount. The excessive dependence of the central bank in their financing should be gradually diminished. Besides, the People's Bank faces difficulties in controlling the seasonal use of funds and ensuring their use from frequent deviations. To provide money for purchasing farm produce, the People's Bank bears the pressure of extended loans. The movement of bank loans along the cycle is made up by the following factors: The funds of the People's Bank of China occupy a dominant position through the whole year, the increase of money supply (M_2) is concentrated on the fourth quarter, and the speed of repaying loans is very slow. As a result, the changes of bank credit in the 1980s aggravated the cyclical fluctuation of economic stopping and starting.

It is necessary to introduce hard budgetary restrictions to specialized banks and reduce their excessive dependence on loans from the People's Bank of China. Banks should not borrow loans from the People's Bank continuously over a long period of time. As the final lender, the People's Bank of China should only meet the demand of short-term loans of commercial banks and the latter's loans to state-owned enterprises cannot exceed the capital of commercial banks. The financing for grain purchases, for instance, should be limited to short-term credit which needs to be returned to the People's Bank of China quickly. Open market business is very useful in this field because it may balance the sudden and unexpected changes in the flow of capital. As to long-term financing, the government must establish new mechanisms to provide capital for key projects outside the traditional channels of bank financing such as entering the capital market directly (or through the state-owned enterprises with good reputation).

(2) Direct and Indirect Instruments of Monetary Policy

Experts hold that the function of monetary policy is determined by the features of economic structure and other factors of economic policy. The key structural factors include the flexibility of price and wages, the extent of economic development, the level and rate of savings and the complexity of the financial market.

The People's Bank of China mainly uses the four instruments of monetary policy: the cash and credit planning, its loan limits to specialized banks, the minimum rate of reserves and the rate of excessive reserves, and its interest rate on loans secured by banks (in a broad sense, including the level and structure of all its decided interest rates of deposits and loans). The first two instruments of policy (the most effective and direct instruments) are used to control the amount of money supply and to distribute loans, thus determining the daily changes of the basic amount of money. The last two instruments of policy exercise their role through changing the cost of funds of the bank and the public (including the depositors and borrowers).

(3) Proposals on Using Direct Instruments of Policy

Some experts have pointed out that after a period of time the People's Bank should use indirect instruments of policy to replace the present control of loans scale. In the 1985-1988 period, the method of distributing loans in China weakened the control over money because the loans were generally motivated by the needs of the sectors of priority and state-owned enterprises and the interest rate was basically without avail in the process of distributing loans. If the central bank relaxes its credit by accommodating one economic sector, why can it not do the same for the other sectors? The exceptions may give rise to a phenomenon of the "law of say", that is, the limit of special loans creates its own demand but finally harms the goal of stabilizing prices by the People's Bank (which happened in 1985 and 1988). To take these reasons into consideration and to escape from the criticism of injustice and favoritism caused by the politicized monetary policy, some countries tried the method of providing subsidies by fiscal channel so as to increase the visibility of chance and choice.

According to foreign experts, the direct supply of loans also produces large negative micro-effects. It restricts the "enterprises culture" development of specialized banks and the adoption of new and more careful management regulations by the People's Bank, and may weaken the reliability and ability of financial intermediaries to pay. From their experiences since 1988, Chinese policy makers have become determined to further deepen the reform and develop more effective and less distorted instruments of policy.

As economic sectors are learning to predict the behavior of government, direct control looses its effectiveness. This phenomenon will be more and more obvious with the further deepening of China's economic reform. Up to now, China has successfully used indirect means of policy to support its economic stability plan and must continue to strengthen this means in the future. With the hard budgetary restriction and the other reform measures, the economic sectors will be more concerned with price changes and the amount of profit, and direct and distorted government interventions will gradually decline. It is impracticable and irresponsible to abolish all direct controls overnight, but this should be put on the agenda of future reforms because there should be a detailed schedule of action about the very important factors of order and speed of transformation.

(4) Proposals on Using Indirect Instruments of Policy
Interest Rate
The following four proposals are mutually related:

a. To simplify the present structure of interest rates, reduce the scope of interest rates for departmental and special loans, gradually abolish preferential interest rates for subsidizing certain departments, regions and enterprises. The better method of providing subsidies are fiscal allocation and transfer.

b. To revise the existing system of fixing all the deposit and loan interest rates by the State Council. This system excludes the price competition among financial institutions. The alternative is: The central bank committee (or the proposed monetary committee) fixes only one basic interest rate and the discount rates of the People's Bank for different periods of time. This interest rate shall be the reference one for all other interest rates which may float within the prescribed limits at the start and float within gradually enlarged limits later.

c. To provide more flexibility for bank competition and permit the banks to collect fees according to the risks involved in loans so as to show the relative efficiency between financial intermediaries. At the beginning a larger floating scope shall be fixed according to the interest rate. When the People's Bank introduces new mechanisms and works out the guidance principles for cautious supervision, the scope of interest rate fluctuations may be extended.

d. To improve the coordination relationship between the income rate of government bonds and the interest rate of fixed bank deposits (for the same period). This may prevent the quick and irregular shift of financial assets which often forces the People's Bank to intervene in support of financial institutions. The sales of treasury bonds by public bidding help the Ministry of Finance fix rational prices through the market mechanism.

Requirements of Reserves
The present system of reserves requires that they must be separately held by each branch of financial institutions and that the deficit part of one branch cannot be made up by the excess part of another branch (except by regular borrowing from inter-

bank financial market). The modernized Chinese payment system and the accounting system centering on the specialized banks enables the People's Bank to further control bank reserves and replace the present system. If it is the need of the monetary situation, the fluctuations of the excess part of reserves should be reduced and the excess part will be transferred to legal reserves. Part of the reserves may become the bonds of the People's Bank; the bonds can constitute the basis of a fund market of the People's Bank and the collateral of specialized banks in the exchange market of banks.

Open Market Operation

The open market operation provides the People's Bank with a major and flexible indirect instrument of policy. Now the People's Bank can handle the rediscount of short-term bonds and manage or issue short-term treasury bonds or its bonds. Part of the loans to the specialized banks issued by the People's Bank can be transformed into a certain form of open market operation; the specific method is to transform the short-term loans distributed to the specialized banks by the People's Bank into bonds.

Organization Strengthened

To raise the analytical ability of People's Bank. In the past ten years or so, the market-oriented reform carried out in China has invested the People's Bank with more responsibilities of managing the economy. It needs to extend the scope of data collection and statistical analysis and raise the technical quality and timeliness. To ensure a firm basis for bank's policy decision, it is necessary to raise the ability of study and research. Remarkable research results are attributed to training and having high-quality research staff to a very large extent. To this the People's Bank should pay great attention.

(5) To Reform and Modernize the Chinese Financial Infrastructure.

Experts hold that in order to enable the Chinese financial system to display its functions, it is important to raise the position of such significant institutions as the People's Bank and the specialized banks, and to accelerate the information work and legal building. Now most of the necessary activities belong to the functions of the People's Bank and a part of them is still under the jurisdiction of the Ministry of Finance. What should be specially pointed out is the need to adjust policies and reinforce the organization building and personnel training in the following fields:

a. To Establish Careful Supervision and Management Systems.

According to some experts, the People's Bank is developing its supervision (audit) ability but has almost no careful management. The present management standard focuses on adapting itself to the requirements of central planned economy rather than ensuring the sound operation of financial institutions. The reform in this field not only requires the drafting of a new framework for careful management but also investing the necessary authority and administrative power in the People's Bank so that it can rectify the unsound operations of financial institutions and lay down stipulations for the loan loss reserve suited to the risks in their composition of assets. The several thousand auditors of the People's Bank need training in the light of the new system. If the present method of direct financial intervention is replaced by an indirect method, this calls for a strong and careful management.

b. To Develop Perfect Accounting Standards.

Many experts hold that the 1985 Law of Accounting authorizes the Ministry of Finance to administer the accounting affairs in the whole country but the ministry has entrusted the People's Bank to administer the practical accounting standards in the financial departments. In a broad sense, the Chinese accounting system is identical to international accounting standards, but does not follow generally accepted accounting pinciples in many key areas. The accounting standards and system have been designed according to the needs of central planned economy and their information system focuses on ensuring agreement with central instructions. This system needs a thorough revision to provide all kinds of necessary information for the policy decision of sound management under the market-oriented economic environment. To realize this goal, the Ministry of Finance has promised to coordinate the general and departmental accounting standards and the enterprise auditing method of China with the international principles. Work has already started.

c. To Develop Management Information Systems.

Only when the following three preconditions are satisfied can the bank effectively collect information from the enterprise departments, help implement the hard budgetary restrictions and improve the allocation of resources. The three conditions are: The banks need to get the most reliable and latest financial information from their clients, have the analytic ability to appraise financial risks, and enjoy full autonomy to choose their clients. Therefore, China has huge amounts of work to do in building organization and training personnel in years to come. The reform of the accounting and auditing systems will raise the information value of financial statements and lay the foundation for the further development of future enterprise and financial reforms.

d. Payment Systems.

Cash is the most important means of payment used by Chinese consumers, and checks mainly by the government organs and enterprises for the clearing only within their cities. Payments between cities and between provinces are completed by mail transfer through the postal system and electronic funds transfer system. China still lacks a nationwide system of check clearing, and there is no definite form of checks. The speed of clearing by check through the clearing center of the People's Bank is very slow because the branches of every bank seem to be independent of their clearing business. This clearing and payment method delays the payment, wastes the money idled in the process of clearing, increases the cost of transactions and restricts the growth of a national banker's market and securities market. People all agree that a modernized payment and clearing system is priority in the modernization of China's financial departments and the People's Bank has made tremendous progress in this respect.

e. To Lay the Legal Foundation for the Development of Financial Departments.

As emphasized by experts, the building of a sound legal system of financial institutions and financial transactions is a key step in financial reform. Urgently needed now are the drafting of a new bank law and the formulation of a new legal article of association for the People's Bank (better enacted separately). They should precisely stipulate the scope of jurisdiction and the basic elements of every business activity. The proposed bank law also has to include some structural factors such as the scope of activities for every financial institution, the standards of entering the market (the most important ones are honesty, experience and minimum capital), merger and change of ownership, and basic careful management (limits on loan concentration and other risks). Clear stipulations are necessary with regard to the autonomy of the People's Bank in enacting and implementing monetary policy, and the type and scope of policy instruments. As no bank can operate in the vacuum, legislation should also include: a law relating to the negotiable financial instruments, the securities law, and the supplementary regulations on the collection of collateral loans. If it is possible, revisions on the Bankruptcy Law should be made (in the light of the practice in China after its promulgation).

(6) To Readjust the Organizational Structure and Scope of Functions of the People's Bank

The organizational structure of People's Bank includes 2,431 subordinate units--a head office, 44 provincial branches (one in each of the 30 provinces and one in each of the 14 cities which have an independent plan), 310 prefectural and city branches, 1,964 sub-branches and 26 offices. This structure is more suited to the exercise of the unique bank function before the reform and the implementation of the central mandatory plans (such as credit, cash and foreign exchange) by the branches of the bank. The structure of People's Bank also indicates its functional position of business manager rather than that of careful supervisor.

Although there are sufficient reasons to enact and implement the fairly tight centralized monetary policy and get rid of the administrative intervention by local (provincial) governments, the large number of management (operating) functions of the People's Bank still need to be decentralized. Once the proposed new functions of the People's Bank are adopted, there will be adjustments in its branches and sub-branches and the assignments of staffs. Especially when the People's Bank shifts its audit function to strengthening the risk management of financial institutions, this will call for the corresponding adjustment in organization and the retraining and relocation of staff. The audit department of the People's Bank should continue to supervise the bank's implementation of credit plan and this may conflict with its new responsibility of careful supervision. This potential conflict may demand further reorganization of structure.

Owing to these reasons, experts have proposed that the People's Bank should gradually reduce the number of its branches and sub-branches and that the set-up of branches and sub-branches in the provinces should be reorganized based on economic areas instead of administrative areas. The reorganized branches and sub-branches of the People's Bank along this line will help strengthen the bank's independence from the relevant provincial and other local governments. With the enhanced independence of the People's Bank, it needs a national People's Bank committee of representative character to collect the experiences from various areas. The presidents of some regional branches will be members of the committee on a rotation basis and their participation will raise the position of information collection center of the reorganized branches. The economic development of China will gradually expand the differences between areas and between departments, so this function will become increasingly important. Like the other big nations, every new branch should have its survey and research department to collect economic data and analyse the trend of economic development in its area.

The original branches of People's Bank can best perform the following functions: cash allocation, clearing, information, collection of data and initial analysis, and community relations. However, the branches are entirely prohibited from making any important decisions on credit and foreign exchange. As the financial reform has changed the functions of the People's Bank, its regional and national organization structures and functions also need changes accordingly.

2. Mobilization of Funds

1) Features of Funds

In the 1983-1988 period, the GDP of China rose at an annual average of 11 percent and its amount of savings went up from 31 percent to 39 percent of the GDP, reaching one of the highest savings rate in the world. At the same time, family savings have increased its proportion in the savings structure. This notable change shows the rapid income rise of rural and urban families. Besides, the quick growth of the economy encourages bank savings to exceed other forms of savings (although the real interest rate from 1984 to 1989 was very low and even negative), thus enormously enlarging the deposits and providing many business chances for both new and old financial institutions.

As a result, M_2 (cash plus current and fixed deposits) rose rapidly and it constituted 37 percent of the GDP in 1979, 69 percent of the GDP in 1988 and surpassed 84 percent in the end of 1990. The assets of financial intermediaries (including specialized banks, financial institutions and insurance companies) were 89 percent of the GDP in 1985, went up to 101 percent in 1988. In the 1985-1988 period, the negotiable securities increased from 3.2 percent to 7.7 percent of the GDP. All the financial assets (including all kinds of bonds and securities) rose from 93 percent of the GDP in 1985 to 113 percent of the GDP in 1988.

China's M_2/GDP ratio is very high. Compared with countries with similar levels, the "deepening" degree of finance in China is surprising and has high liquidity. This high liquidity is very common in countries practising planned economy, which may raise some major questions: Does the high liquidity reflect the "money surplus" derived from involuntary rations and involuntary savings accumulation on the commodity market? Or does it reflect the lack of choice of the families whose investment structure has insufficient assets of weak liquidity? The answers to these questions rest on the effects of proper policies.

Owing to the shortage of consumer goods and people's low income in the years before the reform, most of the small amount of family savings were involuntary. With the enormous increase of consumer goods, the growth of the economy and the new influencing of the prices by market forces, the rise of family savings increasingly shows the people's voluntary choice. This change can be proved by the quick increase of net savings when value-guaranteed savings deposits were launched in the 1988-1989 period. Owing to the pact that inflation declined at a faster rate than people expected in 1990 and 1991, the real interest rate went up and value-added savings deposits rose rapidly. Although there was serious imbalance in the real estate market, a major branch of fixed assets, the relatively serious problem of "currency surplus" has been lessened.

The limited "menu" (financial instruments and periods) of Chinese financial institutions and financial assets, therefore, becomes more important in implementing the government's policy. The banks make up the main part of China's financial system and their assets occupy about 87 percent of the total financial assets. The banks all have big national networks with 122,460 branches and sub-branches, and 12 million staff members. The urban and rural credit cooperatives (providing basic savings and credit business) also have 61,839 branches and sub-branches, and 556,703 staff members. The giant system and rapidly expanding organizations explain why, in periods of quick income increases, China scored successes in financial growth and the high fluidity of bank deposits.

2) Diversification of Financial Instruments

The Chinese financial intermediaries have very successfully mobilized savings, but the large amount of short-term bank deposits caused worry over their stability by people. Although the deposits are still "tigers in the cage", any unforeseen aggravation of inflation may touch off people queuing up to withdraw bank deposits, increasing their excessive demand for durable consumer goods, and rushing to buy goods as happened in 1988. To prevent such phenomena of imbalance, the real positive interest rate must be maintained and new financial instruments developed by the bank. The character of these instruments are decided by the direction of development of the main Chinese financial institutions. For example, if the all-embracing banking principle is chosen to build up financial institutions, the banks will provide securities, insurance, leasing and a wide range of financial services, thus helping diversify the financial instruments. However, only by further developing the housing and securities markets and institutional investors (retirement pension funds and insurance companies) in China, can the investing period be prolonged and the structure of huge family savings be diversified. At the same time, the national networks of specialized banks may be used to sell the long-term bonds of the Ministry of Finance.

With the enlarged business scope of specialized banks and the establishment of newly integrated bank and non-bank financial institutions, China's financial reform has promoted competition in the banking business. However, the competition among financial institutions through prices is still hindered by the following measures: loan limits, the continued adoption of fixed interest rates by administrative orders, directional loans, restriction on competition in absorbing deposits, and restrictions on competition among the rural and urban credit cooperatives. On the contrary, these measures have promoted non-price competition. These tend to increase the number of business offices and seek high profit business by adopting monopoly means such as "exclusively holding clients" in a sector. As these behaviors hinder the effective mobilization of funds by financial institutions and their effective development of new financial instruments and services, the internal industrial barriers against competition should be gradually removed. Other matters meriting attention include the approval of establishing new Chinese and foreign intermediaries, and further increase of branches of specialized banks so as to strengthen competition and enhance economic results.

China is a big country with a high rate of savings, and has sufficient room to accept new proper shareholding intermediary organizations under supervision. However, if there are no appropriate and strict laws, supervision and a strong legal basis, the expansion of banks and non-bank financial institutions will run against the security and steady development of the financial system. Once the People's Bank of China has upgraded its management ability, the smaller credit organs (rural and urban credit cooperatives) shall be permitted to raise their status and change into banks when they meet the conditions of minimum capital and other requirements. As to the scope of bank business, there should be strict requirements for the actual capital and earnings of the banks, particularly so when they seek for enlarging the scope of financial services. To promote competition, the new organs should be encouraged to engage in banking business and be allowed to continue their not-very-traditional banking business. At this stage, however, the two kinds of businesses should not intersect each other. Before coming into effect of carefully formulated laws, the business limits between financial institutions (barries between the institutions) cannot be loosened, and the banks should not be permitted to invest in non-financial instruments on account of diversifying their assets; or vice versa.

3) Changing the Composition of Balance Sheet

Since the start of reform, the proportion of people's deposits in the total liabilities of the Chinese organizations taking in deposits has gone up rapidly. From 1985 to 1990, the proportion of the deposits bearing the highest interest (the fixed deposits of residents) in the total liabilities of specialized banks rose more than 11 percentage points and that in the rural credit cooperatives increased 18.5 percentage points. To maintain the stability of financial intermediates, they should be allowed to shift this financial cost to the borrowers. Since voluntary loans and policy-oriented loans bear comparatively high risks, the above-mentioned financial cost should include the potential loss. The shift of cost by the bank was not permitted in the past and the level of profit difference (fixed) was artificially increased or decreased by the will of officials.

Owing to the fact that the growth of assets in the bank far exceeds the growth of its capital, the bank has enhanced its leverage tremendously. This gives rise to the problem of sufficient rate of bank capital because in recent years the bank has put aside very little reserve of bad debt from loans and the quality of loan components has continued to decline. Between 1985 and 1990 (the ratio of capital to assets went down from 9.6 to 6.2), the bank capital loss surpassed one-third and made the ratio much below the international standard. The government needs to consider a strategy for increasing capital. The minimum standard of capital not only can effectively strengthen the security and reliability of the bank, but also may restrict its expansion, leverage and ability to mobilize funds.

3. Effective Allocation of Resources

Up to now, China has been very successful in mobilizing its savings but the amount of savings cannot maintain the past high-speed growth in the future. Therefore, economic growth cannot help but rely more and more on the full use of various kinds of funds. To distribute funds effectively, China needs a true capital market. Therefore, the reform of banking system, the most important factor of organization of capital market, becomes the major link in the effective use of funds. Making full use of investment funds is another important condition for effectively allocating resources. Thus China can make improvements in three fields: credit distribution, bank management, and enterprise reform.

1) Credit Distribution

Experts have pointed out that almost every country adopts some methods of direct distribution of credit and hidden interest subsidy, but no country uses them as extensively as China. Like many other countries, China's main argument for the direct distribution of bank loans is that if directional loans are not adopted, the funds for economic development and structural adjustment can hardly flow to the prior industrial sectors and backbone enterprises. This argument is based on the reason that the interference of external factors causes the improper operation of market, thus proving the intervention by government, the non-market force, is necessary. This accidental example normally involves the supply of only certain social commodities, particularly when the supply of a type of commodity constitutes a natural monopoly. Here the needed measure seems to be the redistribution of budgetary funds that are beneficial to subsidizing the construction of infrastructual facilities and unbeneficial to subsidizing consumers and enterprises. This is what China is doing now.

Under other circumstances, funds cannot reach the departments of prior development, either because the distorted price levels damage the ability to earn profit, or because of the lack of proper instruments. The best policy measure to improve the profit-earning ability and attract or obtain more investment is price reform. As to projects for which the bank will not issue loans, financing may be solved through issuing bonds or other long-term securities but not using directional loans, which will aggravate the distortion of the loans. During this stage of reform, loans and temporary loans may continue to be used.

Large amounts of loans to enterprises without considering their profits or losses will produce lower social returns and thereby lead to the seriously mistaken distribution of funds. Moreover, contrary to the will of Chinese policy makers, the continued use of diretional loans may possibly hinder the adjustment of industrial structure. For example, these loans may make some companies produce large quantities of stockpiled commodities. The continued financing of state-owned enterprises with losses will make the bank unable to improve the quality of its loan component and squeeze out the clients who can use the funds effectively. In brief, the direct distribution of loans should be restricted and used with careful consideration and under certain conditions. The present system of planned distribution of most bank loans cannot make a correct decision on how much for a loan issued to a certain economic activity, judging from its relevant return.

The component quality, profit earning ability and capital sufficiency rate of bank loans has deteriorated in the past five years. In spite of the recently announced increase of bad debt reserve of loans, the amount is still too small. The need of reincreasing bank capital is a pressing one. The Ministry of

Finance must accept this principle. It shall allow the bank to put aside bad debt reserve of loan losses, which affects the bank's profit and its capital sufficiency rate, in an amount suited to the actual bad debt and the loan risks and losses rather than assumed or artificial prescriptions. The risks and losses should be determined by the People's Bank of China after consulting the judgment of the management staff of the specialized bank and independently appraising the specialized bank's quality of assets. The real financial position and the real worth of asset composition of a bank can be decided only by relying on the full publicity of its financial statements, practising the new accounting standards and conducting thorough asset appraisal.

To solve the contradiction between the function of commercial intermediaries and the imposed policy-oriented loan in the specialized banks, the World Bank has proposed the separate listing of the two different loans in their balance sheet and their statement of profit and loss. The specialized bank may be given a "free range" within which it decides the loans without government interference and bears the entire responsibility of profit or loss from these loans. Giving more choice to the directional loans, this "free range" will be abolished. Finally a "development fund" formed by budgetary appropriations and the sales of government bonds will put the loans in separate accounts: the state policy-orientated loans will be divided from the loans; the banks will issue loans to the borrowers in accordance with the predecided standards of the borrowers' credit standing and ability to repay the loans. The condition of "commercial loan composition" within the free range will be decided by examining its major operating indices, which becomes the best strategy of introducing certain transparency to the bank's operating efficiency. The separation of loan components at least makes public any new, real and possible losses and will finally signalize or prevent a financial crisis. If the banks and other financial institutions cannot be freed from the forced supply of fiscal financing, Chinese financial reform may possibly fail.

2) Bank Management

The bank is the main credit intermediary, and financial reform aiming at raising its returns cannot but touch the potential contradiction in the policy of directional loans.

The administrative "guidance" runs contrary to the bank's autonomous making of loan terms, independent judgment of extending credit and reduction of risks. The low-interest-bearing preferential loans are contradictory to the bank's goal of making a profit. The present interest subsidy to the industrial sectors of prior development enables every enterprise of these sectors to have the chance to receive a loan with interest subsidy, that is, the whole sector enjoys this subsidy while the bank and the Ministry of Finance make the payment. The interest subsidy is not a satisfactory measure, and the more effective, more inexpensive and reasonable choice is to abolish the preferential loan system and provide direct subsidy through budgetary appropriations.

Directional loans run contradictory to careful supervision and control, but they are the guiding principles of the supervision functions of the People's Bank of China.

Mutual conflict of goals and bank's autonomy: The Chinese specialized bank has dual tasks, being both a commercial bank and a development bank. The ability to make profit and optimized loan component are the driving goals in all financial institutions, but the Chinese specialized banks must follow the government's credit policy to serve the economic and social needs that are often contrary to the bank's vitality. Under the form of contracted operation, the optimized operating goal may provide a framework for bank management in China. Therefore, the policy toward state-owned banks should emphasize financial vitality and rigid budgetary restriction; the improvement of system should concentrate on further strengthening the management of credit risk, enlarging credit autonomy, and achieving more flexibility in deciding the interests of loans and deposits. Only in this way can the specialized banks be transformed into financial institutions of vitality, high efficiency and good credit standing.

During this process the banks have to protect their capital from being affected by loan losses, but first they should thoroughly examine their balance sheets to confirm their assets.

In increasing their new loans, the banks should not risk their capital because any loss will finally be borne by the government. Unless the government agrees to the bankruptcy of a company, the banks cannot carry out an active and initiative loan policy. At the same time, the Chinese law only provides the claimer with limited (or incomplete) legal means to obtain repayment from the debtor by taking back the guarantee, obtaining the commodity and liquidating the collateral.

3) Enterprise Reform

To do a good job in managing state-owned enterprises is the key to state economic reform, and this has become an urgent task of Chinese policy makers. Owing to various reasons, the state-owned enterprises have not yet raised their production efficiency and operating levels. A way is to be found that will let the enterprises enjoy better market competition and at the same time keep the relations of high public ownership. This is a difficult problem. The World Bank put forward many proposals, involving industrial structure, the reform of ownership, and the management method and mechanism of the company, to improve the competition environment. All this indicates that enterprises should be put in a economic environment with low centralized control, less distorted enterprise behavior and the existence of competitiveness, where they are responsible for their own profits or losses.

A possible step to achieve the above proposal is that the enterprise adopts the form of company with limited liability, in which the government's responsibility to the enterprise is only limited to the initial capital input. This will be a major improvement of the present system, under which the government bears the unlimited and non-discriminatory financing responsibility and causes the "soft budgetary restriction" of the enterprise. If the loans to enterprises cannot be properly judged by commercial standards, they will become the government's potential, universal and extra-budgetary debt burdens that should be marked in the above-mentioned separate loan component. Up to now, the limited scope and application of the Bankruptcy Law seriously restrict its role of control in the non-centralized socialist economy, thus resulting in soft budgetary restriction and irresponsibility of enterprises.

The worry of improper loan distribution from scattered bank decisions comes from the present distortion of pricing. Therefore, both financial and enterprise reform must be discussed together. From a long-term view, financial reform cannot be successful without the reform of price system because the present price system gives a "misleading" signal for issuing loans, and enterprise reform carried out in the direction to hard budgetary restriction also calls for enterprises to adjust their production according to market signals. Although the most ideal method is to carry out reform in the three fields at the same time, the delayed price reform and enterprise reform should not become the reason for the delay of financial reform.

To realize and ensure the coordination of departments in financial reform, the World Bank previously proposed the establishment of a senior "leading group". The group plays a special important role in many fields of trans-administrative departments. These fields include: formulating accounting regulations, framing careful regulations of supervision and management, setting up bad debt reserves for loans, coordinating the development of China's government bonds market and the Chinese monetary policy, and especially developing the open market business.

Financial reform and investment returns. The contribution of financial system to economic growth lies in its ability to raise the utilization efficiency of funds, that is, the ability to turn savings into productive investment. With the existence of other factors, the increase of this ability by financial intermediaries will gradually reduce the output capital rate that is now rising.

The proposals for raising the efficiency of loan distribution may be summaried as follows.

The loan distribution should have its choice.

When the loan is used to compensate the market failure of enterprises, there is no subsidy to the loan. It is more beneficial to replace the loans containing fiscal subsidy with loans without subsidy.

As commercial intermediaries, the specialized banks should separate the commercial loans from policy-oriented loans.

The role of distributing interest-bearing loans should be strengthened through tax reform and the introduction of hard budgetary restriction on enterprises.

The chain debts are another form of forced directional loans. They weaken the intermediary role of capital played by the banking system and need to be corrected economically and legally.

The forced implementation of contract and the claims and the disposal of loan guarantees and other collaterals should be guaranteed.

4. Industrial Renovation

Experts have pointed out that output growth can be attributed to the increase of production factors (labor and capital) and productivity. The changes in the use of capital is helpful to raise output; however, according to the experience of the World Bank, productivity is the key to explaining the output growth of every country in the long run. Raised productivity is a motivating force of development. Then, what is the force that pushes up productivity? What contribution can the reform of financial departments make to the growth? Except those with more state features, the increase of productivity is closely related to the technical progress that widely spreads through trade, and direct foreign investment and investment in labor capital. Another is the "quality of the economic environment," particularly the existence or absence of market distortion. We are of the opinon that the potential contribution of the financial system rests in its ability to raise the returns of capital. This ability can not only improve the distribution of new capital, but also helps liquidate the assets locked at low productive uses and puts them in uses with higher social and economic results.

Industrial renovation, in a broad sense, is an urgent task faced by the Chinese policy makers. It raises three separate and closely related problems. Firstly, the building of infrastructural facilities needs to be reinforced, especially that in the cities. This facilities must be designed and financed locally. Secondly, with the maturity of China's industrial structure, the backward production of factories with low returns must be closed down or completely renewed and renovated. Thirdly, with the development of China's more matured high-tech industries, the financial system needs changes. The increasingly mature Chinese industrial economy demands correspondingly mature financial institutions. As the national economy grows, many important projects should be decided and financed locally.

The infrastructural facilities in the old coastal cities of China need renovation. The system of direct investment in infrastructural facilities by fiscal appropriation is no more practicable. Therefore, the following must be established:

The resources of local tax, the tax income, may be designated to improve the infrastructural facilities.

The issue of city bonds, when needed, may be used for the investment in large-type and "bulky" infrastructural facilities. This kind of investment has been practised only when the annual revenue permits.

The most common solution for the above matters is the combined use of property tax and city bonds. The income from selling bonds is used for initial investment, and the income from property tax is exclusively used for repaying bonds. This system is especially effective because it enables the government to recover directly the added value of part of a property that has been produced by the investment in infrastructural facilities. China urgently needs such a system because it needs not only new infrastructural facilities but also the development of capital market promoted by the issue of city bonds.

Industrial transformation attracts a large amount of investment. In the past ten years, this transformation has been financed by surplus funds (profit and depreciation). Owing to the decline of industrial profit rate, however, this source of funds cannot meet present needs. The old enterprises ask for the capitalization of their existing assets, especially their fixed assets, thereby creating financial sources for replacing fixed assets and restructuring. These enterprises also ask for funds based on their future incomes and not on their present profits. This demands expanding financial creation and further development of China's capital market, including the adoption of more flexible financial instruments at the local level.

The starting operation of new technology-intensive departments also needs a flexible capital market. Other countries have also discovered that the development of technology-intensive type also asks flexibility in the company scale. Although big companies sometimes easily become high-tech departments (for example, in Japan), the newly-established small common companies can play more outstanding role in the early period (for instance, in Taiwan and the United States). This means that the financing methods must .be diversified, which enables comparatively small-scale investment but with greater risks to obtain financing. The creation of needed financial instruments may also increase the choice of family investors whose investment is mainly limited to current assets with little risks and low earnings.

To make the capital market flexible, experts suggested the development of new financial instruments, expecially the different kinds of bonds. As the financial system of China is and will still be dominated by banks, there is an urgent need for new financial business and institutions. Especially in Western countries, the business of investment banks and risk investment companies helps the relocation of industrial assets and the financing of high risk projects. The above measures are superior to the present related management mechanism of China in enterprise annex and establishment of new enterprises. Proper methods must be explored to appraise the assets of bankrupt enterprises and merger enterprises, and the shares of losses between the government at different levels and economic entities.

Finally, if there is no enterprise renovation, banking reforms will always face the increasing accumulation of bad debt from loans in the component of bank assets. Therefore, bank and enterprise reform should proceed simultaneously.

Chapter III
The Central Bank

1. Current Situation of the Central Bank

1) Brief and Arduous History

People often call the central bank "one of the greatest inventions in the 20th century." The reason is mainly because the establishment of central bank enables the government to have a proper organization for managing national financial organs and monetary and financial activities, a powerful organization to implement the government's policy of macro-economic control. This role of the central bank is embodied in its three major basic functions: Firstly, as the issuing bank, it monopolizes the issuing of currency. Secondly, as the bank of banks, it opens accounts, provides financing and conducts clearing only for the commercial banks and financial institutions, and performs the function of "final lender." Thirdly, as the bank of the government, it handles the receipt and payment of the national treasury, opens accounts for the government, represents the government in issuing bonds and manages the business of payment of principals and interest, takes care of the state's foreign exchange and gold reserves, interferes in the foreign exchange market on behalf of the government, and extends loans to the government or (indirectly) buys government bonds when necessary.

Based on the above three major functions, the main business of the central bank includes: a. providing a convenient clearing for the banks and various financial institutions; b. examining and deciding the establishment, merger, and dissolution of banks and various financial institutions and establishment of their branches; c. issuing new currency; d. handling discount from and issue loans to the banks and various financial institutions; e. deciding the benchmark interest rate; f. engaging in open market operation (buying or selling government bonds in the open market to increase or decrease the supply of base money); g. deciding the deposit rate of securities transactions (deciding the proportion of cash, not borrowed money, used to buy securities); h. interfering in foreign exchange market; i. studying the macro-economic situation.

The People's Bank of China began to carry out the functions and power of the central bank in 1984. In the early days of its establishment, the central bank did not divide its funds from those of the specialized banks and it made up the deficits caused by more loans than deposits in the specialized banks, this made the central bank unable to control actively the base currency and use effectively its own loans to regulate the total amount of loans in society.

Thus, the central bank put forward in October 1984 a proposal of reforming the control system of funds. Firstly, the funds of central bank should be divided from those of specialized banks. Secondly, the planned loans given to the banks by the central bank each year should be distributed to them according to the plan in advance; when the banks want to borrow from the central bank, the amounts shall be limited to their planned quotas. In this way the central bank can actively control its amount of loans, thus controlling the total amount of social loans indirectly.

This reform is an important measure for the central bank to exercise indirect control. When this reform proposal was put forward in October 1984. The decision had been made that the loans given to the banks the next year in the central plan should be based on the loans issued to them by the central bank at the end of December 1984. As a result, to enlarge the base amount of loans borrowed from the central bank, the banks vigorously granted loans. This was the reason causing uncontrolled credit in 1984 on the part of the banks.

The uncontrolled credit at the end of 1984 gave rise to the high-speed growth of industrial production in 1985. In the first quarter of 1985, industrial production went up 22-25 percent and the total demand rose very repidly. In compliance with the opinion of the government, the central bank carried out a tight monetary policy. It first lowered the foreign exchange reserve and used a part of this reserve to buy durable consumer goods, which were sold to absorb currency from the market. Beginning from April 1985, the central bank reduced its loans and restricted the amounts of loans to the banks, that is using direct control of loans.

After this loan restriction for eight months, the growth rate of industrial production began to decrease from 25 percent in early 1985 to below ten percent in November 1985 and then to 0.9 percent in February 1986. To avoid further decline the central bank gradually loosened its credit in February and March 1986 and changed the means of monetary policy. Except the loans for fixed assets, it abolished the quota control of all other loans and adopted the indirect control method by controlling mainly its own loans.

The time of loosening credit also lasted about eight months, from February to October 1986, and the growth rate of industrial production recovered to above ten percent. The effect of monetary policy in these few years indicated that its time lag is about eight months. If this is a law, it was already eight months from the start of loosening the monetary policy in February to October 1986. At that time, the central bank should adjust its policy and contract its loans properly, but it did not pay attention to studying the time lag of monetary policy. The central bank also had shortcomings in managing its loans in 1986, that is delegating to its branches the control of loans issued by banks in local areas. To express their local tendency and support of local governments to develop economy, the central bank branches wanted to issue more loans, this made the head office of central bank unable to control the central bank's loans actively and effectively, and therefore unable to control the total loans to society. Owing to this reason, the issue of loans was relaxed again in 1986 and the loan rate increased to 27.2 percent, only one percentge point lower than that of 1984, a year when loan issuing was out of control.

The central bank summed up in 1987 the experience of the past few years and improved the means of control, and succeeded in the adjustment and control done by monetary policy in the year. Firstly, it abolished the stipulation that permited its branches to issue loans with a certain proportion of their excess reserves, and unposed quotas on the temporary loans issued by its branches. This concentrated the control power of central bank's loans in the hands of head office. Secondly, strict management of central bank's loans was imposed. For example, the head office instructed its branches strictly to call back the 80 billion yuan of temporary loans in the first half of the year. Of special importance is that the central bank timely noticed that after the second quarter there appeared the tendency of too rapid growth of industrial production and loans. To check the over-heated economic growth, in September the central bank decidedly adopted a series of proper measures of tight control: to control strictly the amount of loans issued by the central bank, to raise the reserve rate of deposits by two percentage points, to increase the interest rate of the loans issued by the central bank, and to absorb 5 billion yuan of special deposits from the rural credit cooperatives.

These measures effectively checked the too rapid growth of loans and the growth rate of loans was 17 percent in 1987, the lowest in recent years. The monetary policy of the central bank was successful in 1987 because it achieved proper contraction and supported the steady economic growth. The success of macro-financial control in 1987 showed the central bank could regulate the economy by using monetary policy and achieve success by indirect means of control.

The central bank originally decided to continue the monetary policy of proper contraction in 1988. However, the series of policy measures of the Central Committee of the Chinese Communist Party and the State Council at that time promoted the high-speed growth of industrial production. In the first and second quarters industrial production rose at the rate of 17 percent and industrial loans also went up rapidly, four times that of the same period in the previous year. At the start of the year, the central bank decided to call back 25-80 billion yuan of its temporary loans in the first six months of the year but actually called back only 0.4 billion yuan. Presented with this situation, the central bank faced a serious contradiction. If it firmly adhered to the original tight monetary policy, it should have adopted forceful measures such as calling back the central bank's temporary loans, contracting credit, restricting the total demand of society and preventing inflation. But the central bank did not have the right of independently deciding the monetary policy, when the government did not instruct the central bank to check the over-heated economy, the central bank had no power to make the decision of practising tight credit. As a result, it passively adapted itself to the overheated economic growth and actually carried out the expansion of the monetary policy.

The passive character of central bank is also shown in adjustments of the interest rate policy. In early 1988 the central bank proposed to raise the interest rate on bank deposits and loans so as to maintain the amount of savings deposits, prevent the rush to withdraw money from banks and resrict demand. Because the adjustment of interest rates involves the interests of different fields, the State Council delayed its decision. It was not until September when people successively rushed to withdraw bank deposits and buy commodities, that the State Council approved the central bank to raise interest rates and offer interest rates of ensured value on savings deposits. This missed the important time to raise interest rates.

The tight credit measures were imposed in September 1988. In August 1988 the price index of retail sales grew 23.7 percent, the rush to buy goods appeared repeatedly on the market, the economy was overheated and the market was unstable. So the State Council decided to adopt an austere policy. Beginning from September 1, 1988, the central bank adopted austere measures: to reduce enormously the limits on the loans issued by the banks and strictly control the targets, raise the reserve by one percentage point, increase the interest rate on deposits and loans, and ensure the value of residents fixed savings deposits for a period of over three years. Instead of increase, the loans issued by the banks decreased 600 million yuan in the three months from September to November when industry and agriculture needed money. As a result, the serious shortage of cash for buying farm and sideline products forced the purchasing department to give farmers I. O. U. slips, the banks held the exchange differences between themselves, and enterprises universally defaulted. Then the central bank increased its loans by over 60 billion yuan in December. In the four months from September to December, the whoel banking system increased more than 60 billion yuan of loans, 100 percent and 60 percent less than the increases in the same period of 1986 and 1987 respectively. This indicated the effect of strong austerity.

The central bank continued its contracting policy in 1989. The austere monetary policy from September 1988 to June 1989 produced the effect that the high rate of industrial growth went down to below ten percent. The increase rate of social retail sales decreased to 8.8 percent in June and negative growth in August, and the market became sluggish. Judging from the experience of past few years, the time lag of monetary policy stands at about eight months. From the start of the austerity in September 1988 to June 1989 it lasted eight to nine months; the sluggish market appeared and unemployment rose.

Therefore, the monetary policy should have been adjusted by properly relaxing credit at the end of the second quarter or the start of the third quarter of 1989. Public opinion at that time held that austerity had not reached the end and that although there appeared sluggish market, the social total demand exceeded the social total supply and continued austerity was still needed. As the government had no intention of adjusting the policy, the central bank adhered to the tight monetary policy. Industrial production continued to decline in September and October—the growth rate was 0.9 percent in September and negative in October. Then the central bank began in October to ease the credit according to the will of government. The austerity lasted 13 months from October 1988 to October 1989. Judged from both the actual economic life and the law of monetary policy, it was too late for the central bank to adjust the monetary poicy in October 1989.

The central bank began to loose the control of its credit in October 1989 and continued to do so in the whole year of 1990.

The loans rose 22 percent in 1990, a fairly high rate in recent years. Moreover, this rate tremendously surpassed the addition of industrial growth rate (six percent) and price index growth rate (two percent) in 1990. Why did this situation come into being? It was partially because the rich harvest in 1990 needed increased funds to buy farm and sideline products and the policy-oriented loans also needed funds. An important reason was that under the conditions of sluggish market and insufficient effective demand, the leading departments and enterprises continued to increase production despite the lack of market for their commodities. As a result, a considerable amount of the commodities produced were stockpiled in warehouses, occupying a large part of loans.

The reason of creating large stockpiled products lay in the fact that some departments asked for the relaxing of monetary policy to prevent the decline of production and promote the factors of economic growth but did not acknowledge the lack of effective demand. As a result the adjustment and increase of effective demand were neglected when the policy was adjusted. At the same time, to protect the existence of some enterprises, the bank still provided them with loans although their products had no market.

The State Council proposed in March and April the increase of fixed asset investment to regulate the effective demand. In December the banking system issued large amount of fixed asset loans by settling the "chain debts" and these loans in that month rose to 15.8 billion yuan, an increase of 12 billion yuan over that of the same period in 1989. The banking system continued to make these loans in 1991. Their amount totaled 46.9 billion yuan from January to September, 29.2 billion yuan over that of the same period in the previous year, and the loans for industrial circulating capital went up less than those of 1990. The increased fixed assets loans played a positive role in regulating the effective demand and stimulating the sluggish sales.

Since September 1988 the central bank has adopted the direct control method in its monetary policy, that is using targets to control the loans issued by different banks, and this method has continued to be used up to the present time. At the same time, to shift the emphasis of loans to large and medium-sized enterprises, the central bank and the industrial leading departments jointly listed the names of enterprises and the amounts of their loans and instruct specialized banks to issue loans to them, that is the method of directional loans.

2) Present Outstanding Contradictions of Central Bank; Unclear Duties and Resposibilities, Doing Concrete Specialized Business, Dual Purposes of Monetary Policy, and Defects of Profit-Sharing System

Experts hold that there have been many questions to study since the establishment of central bank.

(1) The central bank still engages in some (although not many) business activities directly related to enterprises.

The businesses include those that should be undertaken by the central authorities such as loans to the old revolutionary base areas, national minority areas, and border and poor areas as well as commercial loans to a small number of enterprises. It also includes loans under the instruction from the above such as those for buying farm and sideline products, those for buying export commodities and commercial loans to enterprises. The main reasons are:

a. Branches of the central bank, from highest to lowest, should naturally be located in cities. Since the banks' operational facilities, such as office buildings, telecommunications, transportation, living quarters, water, power and food supplies, have to be provided by the municipal government, so, if the central bank fails to provide them loans, all these facilities can hardly be available. As bank employees say, "We have to offer some road-paving money to maintain our normal activities."

b. Intervention from the local government: Some loans, especially non-policy-oriented ones "from directives" are not offered at first by local branches of the central bank. In the local economy, a local government plays an increasingly important role, and often presses the bank to fund a number of local construction projects. Since the local branches are under the dual leadership of their head office and the local governments, they are often compelled to supply funds themselves or order their specialized banks to do so.

c. Some capitals and loans should originally be allocated and supplied by state finance or by policy-specialized banks, such as capital granted to old liberated-areas, national minority regions, border and undeveloped areas, loans for policy-permitted-losing enterprises, loans for purchasing farm and sideline products, exported products, for key infrastructural constructions. However, as our state finance has difficulties to provide these capitals and loans and policy-oriented banks are not yet available, the majority of the funds used for the above purposes can only be provided or borne directly by the central bank.

From the above analysis, it is not difficult to seek a solution: a. the first two points (a. and b.) are of similar nature, and are connected to the local governments' intervention. So the way out mainly depends on how the governments at all levels convert their functions. What is more important is that the local governments must sever themselves from the enterprises subordinate to them by relieving themselves from their obligations to supply funds. b. Policy factors compelling the central bank to give ordinary loans must be removed. If a fund should originate from fiscal allocation, let state finance be responsible, and if loans should be given on preferential conditions, the business should be transferred over to policy banks.

Obviously, the solution to all these problems cannot be accomplished overnight. Nevertheless, the government must set a solid goal and create conditions for their solution instead of intensifying them.

(2) Comments on the central bank's profit-retaining system

Some experts advocate that the central bank should not be a profit-making concern. Others hold that although non-profit-making is one of the characteristics distinguishing the central bank, we must never deny the fact that in its performance, the central bank is normally producing profits. So the key point is how to distribute the profits. For bank reform, let us take the U.S.A. as a yardstick. Revenues of the Federal Reserve Bank

(FRB)—the US central bank—consists of incomes from holders of various securities, loans from member banks and incomes from discount transactions. In recent years, its net income after expenditure stands at as high as US$10 billion, the majority of which was in the hands of FRB. People therefore did not question that as FRB generated a high income it would act as an independent central bank, beyond the bounds of the government's budget. The same also happens in countries with a developed market economy. It is necessary for the bank to retain part of the profits it has created in order to enable the central bank to maintain certain independence and its employees to enjoy a comparatively high income, thus attracting talented people to work in the central bank and encouraging them to perform well. Of course, for the sake of enhancing its efficiency, the bank should keep its setup in line with the requirements of the market economy and its staff reduced.

Nowadays, people, talking about the present pattern of the central bank, are often in favor of setting up branches according to economic zones instead of the administrative regions. Theoretically speaking, this is correct. But two points must not be ignored: a. At present it seems that only the United States and Germany have their central banks established not in accordance with administrative regions and both are subject to federal systems. b. Restructuring of the central bank following the pattern as suggested needs a higher level of management. Therefore, it takes time. Virtually, the purpose of severing links of the central bank's local branches with administrative regions is to minimize the intervention of the administrative authorities, especially local government's interference in the bank's business. This can be realized in the following ways: to transform government's functions and limit credit-allocating power of the central bank's local branches.

In restructuring the central bank, experts hold that the top priority is to reform its macro-regulation mechanism. This means that we should transform, as quickly as possible, the present regulation mechanism characterized by a direct allocation of credit according to administrative regions to an indirect regulation mechanism, which relies mainly on controlling the volume of currency and interest rate, supplemented by the control of credit. To carry out this transformation, it is imperative to standardize our deposit reserve system, remodel the re-lending system and focus lendings mostly on discount loans instead of credit loans. Moreover, we should handle, as early as possible, open market business, set up security deposit money systems and create a mechanism with the interest rate to be decided by the market, etc.

(3) Improving the central bank's structure and intensifying its functions.

It is also advocated by the experts that the central bank itself should transform its functions. It should hand over to the policy banks all ordinary banking business, such as lendings for specialized items, restore the nature of the People's Bank of China as a managing agency, and run the People's Bank as a central bank in its real sense.

It must be persistent in reversing the trend of using bank funds as fiscal allocations. To keep the currency stable this should be regarded as priority for the central bank; financial overdraft, preferential loans in the nature of financial subsidies and remitted loans must absolutely be prohibited as such should have fallen to the categories of state finance.

The authority of the central bank in policy-manipulating must be reinforced. Its policy-manipulation should rest on comparatively long-time results and efficiency of the macro-economic regulation instead of being confined to short-term economic conditions and partial interest. In addition, the central bank must stress stability, continuity and independency of its policies.

Besides, the central bank must establish its legal status, and steer and govern finance and banking in accordance with the law. There should be explicit legal norms for the central bank to exercise its duties, rights and conduct, which are effectively protected by law.

Some experts also propose improvements, as quickly as possible, to the central bank's macro-regulation means. Since the establishment of the central bank system in China, the People's

Bank starts to keep eyes on the macro-regulatory means. Legal and economic means, such as legal deposit reserve system, re-lending system, re-discount system and interest rate system, are being adopted. As evidenced in practice the adoption of these systems has strengthened the central bank's functions of macro-regulation, though the scope of operation is small, and weak in strength, due to the predominance of planned management. Therefore, the following suggestions may be useful: a. Deposit reserve systems at different levels should be established for all types of financial institutions or different regions so that varied rates for deposit reserves can be applied. It is also suggested that the deposit reserve rate of the commercial banks be higher than that of the policy banks and that in the developed areas, higher than the backward areas. b. Central bank's re-discount business should be expanded and re-discount proportion in the central bank's base currency input be elevated, in order to promote the development of the discount and re-discount market. c. The central bank's re-lending management system should be improved. The central bank ought to shift its present practice of lending loans mainly to managing offices of specialized banks to its operational banks. Meanwhile, the central bank must decentralize its loan-making power to its branches in cities. As for re-lending, it is also suggested to bring about a change on the current form of lending on credit to that on mortgage and re-discount. d. Open market operations be transacted, and securities trading be undertaken by the central bank through financial market so as to regulate market currency circulation. e. The interest rate control system should be improved by setting up a floating rate system focused on re-lending (re-discount) rate. As to the rate of the commercial banks, the central bank needs only to take care of the ceiling on deposit and the minimum base of the loan.

(4) Prompt unification of the objective of monetary policy

The objective of China's monetary policy is invariably aimed at "developing economy and stabilizing currency." However, the macro-regulation exercised by the central bank in recent years often resulted in conflicts between "developing economy" and "stabilizing currency," the former bringing about the sacrifice of the latter. This state, if not reversed in time, will not only affect the central bank's macro-regulatory orientation, but also jeopardize the advance of the socialist market economy. So the central bank must stick to the unified thinking of simultaneously developing economy and stabilizing currency, uphold economic expansion on the basis of economic results and firmly resist the quantity-type growth, which brings no economic benefit. Besides, a serious attitude must be taken by the central bank towards currency-issuing plan, which, after being approved by the National People's Congress every year, should be strictly observed and enforced. No unit or individual should have the right to act otherwise.

2. On the Relative Independence of the Central Bank

1) Why Does the Central Bank Need Independence?

In the opinion of some experts, the fundamental principle of the independence of the central bank lies in the fact that what politicians and government authority hanker after is inconsistent with a continuous anti-inflationary policy. Thus, arrangements should be made within the system to let the formulating and enforcing of monetary policies concur on a single organization independent of the government. Only by this means will the disciplines of monetary policies be best guaranteed.

2) What Kind of Independence Is Needed by the Central Bank?

Some people argue that the central bank and its officials should not be accorded too much power whereas others contend that far too little consideration is given to the independence of the central bank, especially in establishing its independent status in practice. If the central bank, as a money-issuing bank, is not given an independent position, how can the principle of issuing money be observed economically? And in the absence of observance, how can the stability of the issued money value be maintained? Financial policy is formulated by the government and if a deviation appears in the economy, the nation's financial policy will inevitably deviate with it. When the central bank fails to be the sole authentic institution to regulate money circulation, how can it be expected to control inflation? In China, the central bank is under the direct administration of the State Council and so is directly controlled by the government. As mentioned earlier, government policies are geared to economic development. So, if lacking independence itself, the central bank will more often than not blindly follow in the footsteps of the government. This has been so for some years past, in granting loans or issuing money. Government departments or government authorities at different levels succeed in obtaining loans by pressing the central bank, which cannot break free from this pressure mechanism and thus cannot withstand administrative pressures from various quarters.

Experts believe that the independence of the central bank can be placed under the leadership of the government. The central bank should establish coordinative and cooperative relations with the government. It should give support to the government's economic policies provided that they don't impair monetary stability. The most important responsibility on the part of the bank is to control the amount of hard cash in circulation and not to allow random increase made by the government at will. Of course, the central bank must cooperate with the government, but within a certain limit, i.e. to maintain the stability of hard cash. For example, if the government requires the central bank to buy bonds, the latter should refuse as this is tantamount to issuing more paper money. The central bank should operate on its own decisions but within the government's internal mechanism. Nevertheless, the central bank and the government have different aims with the former aiming at stabilizing the value of money and prices while the latter, due to political reasons, is focused on economic growth. Coordination between the two is advised. If successful, the nation will greatly benefit by it. However, if the government should refuse suggestions concerning money or price stability from the central bank, it would mean a tremendous loss to the nation.

3) The Relative Independence of the Central Bank Be Maintained

How should the independent status of the central bank be consolidated? Experts hold that this can be achieved institutionally. a. The head office of the People's Bank should shift from under the direct control of the State Council to the position of being responsible to the National People's Congress (NPC) and its Standing Committee, putting it under the latter's leadership and supervision. The People's Bank of China shall report at regular or irregular intervals to the Standing Committee in specific and statistical form regarding its financial position, targets of monetary policy, amount of issued money in circulation, interest rate and credit policy and subject them all to the latter's scrutiny. The People's Bank of China shall carry out vertical management on all its branches and subsidiary offices so as to avoid administrative interference from local authorities. b. Pertinent laws shall be enacted to clearly stipulate the authority and functions of the central bank and to ensure the independence of its activities. c. The central bank shall decide on the amount of money in circulation based on the trends of economic development and execute the decision after it has been approved by the NPC. After approval it shall be enforceable by law. Without the majority agreement of the NPC Standing Committee, the money to be issued shall not exceed the decided amount. Meanwhile, it shall be stipulated by law that fiscal deficits will not be covered by overdrawing from the central bank. The Chinese central bank has currently done many of things connected with commercial banking, not conducive to heightening its position as a policy-making authority. Instead, these activities disperse its energy and play down its key functions. Therefore, the central bank ought to consciously focus its energy on major tasks but keep aloof from such practical matters as special loans (so-called symbol of power) and refer them to other financial institutions for help.

In the opinions of experts, the independence of a central bank rests on the strength of its monetary policy, the major objective of which is to achieve monetary stabilization to sustain economic growth. Some people hold that "inflation" begets "compulsory savings," which can be used as investment to promote economic growth. Some Latin American countries are just following this policy—-making use of "inflation" to do construction work. What is the result? Let us compare Venezuela with Taiwan: The former hit a per capita income of US$ 500 while the latter reached US$ 100. Taiwan was seeking development from stability, but Venezuela by inflation. Now the per capita income in Taiwan is US$ 7000-8000, and yet in Venezuela the figure only US$ 1000-2000.

If the monetary policy of a central bank is not to stabilize currency, this will make the policy restrictive one moment and relaxed the next, the economy prosperous today and depressed tomorrow. It is unnecessary for a stable monetary policy to be contracted. The central bank tended to be relaxed first in a policy that was liable to expand to the extreme, and then tighten up all of a sudden, thereby giving rise to an inevitable change in the policy. This is very unfavourable to the economy.

The South Korea monetary policy, which was subordinate in the 1960s-1970s to its government policy of economic growth, was expansionary. Subsequent governments brought the inflation rate from 20 percent down to 5 percent through a tight policy of price stabilization in the 1980s. The South Korea monetary policy of the 1960s-1970s was somewhat similar to the Chinese one in the mid-1980s, the difference being a micro-base in South Korea where the micro-mechanism is of self-restraint, therefore, enterprises have to bear the risk of investment if they wish to expand. But currently Chinese enterprises fall behind in this mechanism, so an expansionary monetary policy will bring about an even more severe aftermath in China.

A monetary policy is essentially a controlling one, and its aim is restrain or limit the availability of funds so that the amount of funds absorbed by the society can be commensurable to the funds available under the circumstances of not jeopardizing price stability and overall economic balance. Hence the contradiction below. To keep prices stable, the monetary authorities strive to bring the availability of funds under control; to attain economic growth, the authorities become a fund provider. Can the central bank's monetary policy exercise these two functions at the same time? Of course not. Therefore, the monetary policy should pursue a unitary objective and that is price stability.

The range of the objective of a monetary policy is closely related to the independence of the central bank. If the currency is endowed with a unitary and definite objective, i.e., price stabilization, then the central bank will have its express responsibility, right and, greater independence. Otherwise, the central bank differs little from other government departments and has hence negligible independence. Therefore the unitary and definite objective of monetary policy and the independence of the central bank are mutually complementary and also indispensable for monetary and economic stability. Meanwhile the monetary policy should coordinate other economic policies of the government and support these policies by ensuring price stability. In addition, the monetary policy shall be practised in tandem with other policies, such as a fiscal policy which is very important as the fiscal balance in Japan, Taiwan and Singapore contributes immensely to maintaining low inflation.

It is also essential to build up a mechanism to supervise the monetary policy for its effective execution. This mechanism requires that the governor of the central bank realize the objective of his policy pronounced within his tenure of office, submit a semi-annual policy statement to the premier and an annual report of its execution to the congress before the governor's official achievements are audited by an outside agency convened by the premier. Supervision over the monetary policy can also be exercised by pronouncing the target of monetary aggregate. The establishment of regulations for supervising monetary policy is not merely to assure the public of clarity and maintain it, but also to ensure the motive force whereby the central bank can hit the target it has pronounced.

4) China Must Set Up a Monetary Committee

In the opinion of many experts, it is necessary for China to set up a monetary committee or a committee of its central bank to ensure the independence of the bank itself as well as to make its independence commensurate with its economic policy. As a standing committee, it would do its best to solicit comments and suggestions from all quarters and incorporate a panel of economic and technical experts. This committee has the right with the permission of the State Council to make quick decisions about such key economic variables as interest rate and credit instruments.

To keep prices and economy stable, China calls for a powerful central bank whose prestige, dignity, strength and independence will rest with its managerial level, and only if it shows its actual ability in working out and practising monetary policy, can it win the support and trust of the public and make the government delegate authority to it.

To improve the central bank's professional ability, the essential point at present is: the People's Bank must broaden its scope, improve its quality and timeliness in respect of data collecting and statistics analysis, and to enhance its ability to study and analyze. The experience of Japan, South Korea and other countries and regions has indicated that an able research department will provide the central bank with timely and valuable suggestions as to the tendency of economic growth while outstanding research achievement hinges to a great extent upon the nurturing and the enlisting of high-level research fellows.

3. Some Relationships to Be Properly Handled by the Central Bank

1) The Relationship Between Direct and Indirect Regulation and Control

Experience in banking worldwide has shown that, the means of direct regulation and control works in developing countries, but that of indirect regulation and control holds good also for developed countries. Therefore, the experience must be assimilated in the light of the specific national conditions. Although unable as yet to divorce itself entirely from direct regulation and control at present, China has to follow gradually the way of indirect regulation and control.

2) The Relationship Between Monetary Policy and Economic Development

A correctly formulated and effectively implemented monetary policy rests eventually with its support of economic development as well as to the raising of the people's living standard. China now works out a monetary policy, the main purpose of which is to stabilize currency. It usually happens, however, that the central bank tends to be saddled with the double task of ensuring monetary stabilization and economic development. Therefore, to study the objective of monetary policy we should not focus only on the bank but also on the fiscal question, which is more important. In the meantime, the enterprise should independently make its own decisions and be solely responsible for its own profits and losses, as the central problem is how to realize economic results.

3) The Relationship Between Directional Loan and Independent Bank Operation

The precedent is available with governments in various countries to develop their economies with directional loans in the burgeoning period, but this is uneconomical. With economic growth, the directional loan will, due to restrictions, taper off until cancellation. The problem facing China today is how to pare away this kind of loan and exercise management on separate accounts or establish special management organs. Even if they are policy-oriented loans, banks should be given the authority to grant such loans on their own with the source of funds obtained through fiscal measures.

4) The Relationship Between the Head and Branch Offices of the People's Bank

Owing to the possible existence of the monetary expansion of the People's Bank influenced by local authorities, it is necessary to set up, according to economic regions, five or six branches of the central bank to be presided over by presidents directly designated by Beijing, thereby reducing local government influence in monetary policy. This also contributes to financial integration and the abolition of regional separation.

4. The Directional Loan

As held by experts, the term of the directional loan has a certain policy-oriented connotation. According to principle, it will be more effective to materialise the directional loan by virtue of taxation or other subsidy methods. Failure to do so fiscally, the performance of the loan will be restricted to some extent.

In the World Bank's experience, resources were erroneously distributed in many nations as a result of the directional loan granted to them. The loan in these countries failed to go, contrary to the original intention of the loan makers, to the industrial sections in need but instead gave rise to a host of problems, such as corruption and the irrational use of resources. Due to certain political reasons, matters will grow more complicated and serious. This does not mean that the policy-oriented loan is incorrect in its amount, but its success has to hinge on some other conditions: a. effective management of the directional loan by the government; b. very low subsidy; c. the decision-making power of the bank granting the loan so that it can be sure of the enterprises and projects in dire need of loans; d. normal policy-oriented environment on which enterprises rely for their existence. If, however, all these conditions can be met, there will be no need for directional loans.

As far as China is concerned at present, what policy-oriented loans are appropriate or correct, and what are not as well as what should be currently approved in China, solutions to the above may not be so simple as imagined. The loans awarded to some loss-making state-owned enterprises will constitute a threat to the reform of Chinese financial structure and considerable troubles may possibly ensue later on, as the loans have mainly been granted to enterprises with low efficiency rather than those with good performance. In the entire Chinese structure, there exists some pressure, coming chiefly from such considerations as social stability, since the state-owned enterprises take full responsibility of their staff and workers. Not making loans to these enterprises will cause much trouble to social stability. In Taiwan and South Korea, loans made to small enterprises are meant to bring them to the field of international trade. Taiwan and South Korea, being geographically smaller, principally rely on developing export-oriented economies. China's mainland differs with its vast area and more sophisticated cases. But what is worth considering is that to solve the matter with fiscal subsidy may be better than with the directional loan.

Two major problems lie ahead for China: a. Although necessary, the scope of the directional loan should be restricted rigorously, for instance, it can be made in housing, pollution prevention and high-technology. But our current directional loans are wide-ranged involving our purchasing agricultural and side-line products, solution of our enterprises' difficulties and more so our energy, communications, and the construction of raw materials. All this must be improved. If not, grave consequences may possibly arise. Of course, the government sometimes needs to run risks. Neither public nor private enterprise can escape that. In the absence of the correct choice of the directional loan, defeat will possibly ensue, and if the loan is appropriately selected, even the state-owned enterprises will likewise attain substantial achievements. b. In the final analysis the directional loan in developing countries should be eliminated. What conditions are called for? Are there any conditions available in China for the purpose? What measures we need to take in China's reform of its financial structure? All this merits conscientious study. We can perhaps say that the directional loan will be removed if sufficient funds are obtainable from social bases and our basic industries can run automatically. We must stress one thing here: a large number of projects, if incorrectly selected by the government, would lead to the building of many imperfect enterprises being operated at a loss for a long time. These long-term loss-making enterprises will press the bank for a directional loan. If so, although subjectively attempting to shake off the directional loan, the government will find it by no means an easy job to extricate itself from such loans.

Chapter IV
Capital Market

1. An Overview of China's Capital Market

China's capital market is growing fast.

Over the past decade or so, the swift progress of financial system reform and the deepening of the urban and rural economic reform have prompted a sharp increase in family savings deposits, thereby promoting the rapid growth of capital market in China. In the meantime, the number of new-type financial organizations has increased enormously in direct competition with the traditional means provided by the state-owned banking system. The further development and change of financial institutions and financial assets during the last several years have greatly expanded the scale and influence of China's capital market. Since treasury bonds were issued in 1981 for the first time, the development of the capital market has followed a beaten track, successively issuing government bonds, special bonds, enterprise debentures and local government bonds as well as stocks. The stocks were issued under special circumstances in the absence of a corporation law and of a legal basis to protect the individual's title to the assets of enterprises. Participants in the capital market include individuals, state-owned banks, trust and investment corporations, state-owned enterprises and their pension funds. Because the People's Bank of China imposes strict requirement for reserves, insurance companies are not permitted to hold securities. During the ten-year period, 1981-1991, the securities floated by the government totalled 140 billion yuan and the outstanding balance of government securities at the end of 1991 stood at about 85 billion yuan. The amount of other issued securities, inclusive of enterprise debentures and stocks, approximated 70 billion yuan. About over 40 billion yuan worth of securities can present-ly be traded at secondary markets. Treasury bonds now occupy a large proportion on the capital market, but an equal portion is composed of the other remaining financial bonds (such as bonds floated by banks or trust and investment companies), bonds of state-owned investment corporations (long-term construction bonds), debentures and a small amount of stocks (strictly speak-ing, these stocks are chiefly preferred stocks rather than common stocks).

Since the establishment of the securities exchanges in Shen-zhen and Shanghai, the trading of stocks has been unprecedent-edly brisk and significant changes have been effected in the transactions on secondary markets. The stock exchanges have replaced the dominant position once held by the transactions of treasury bonds (accounting, in the aggregate, for 99% of the trading volume in 1987). Once new stocks go public, the trading volume is expected to grow. At these two securities exchanges, more than 100 stocks can be traded in public, and dealings over the counter started in December 1990. A securities dealers' com-puterized automated quotation and transaction network has formed, a network connecting several cities with its controlling center in Beijing. After a period of time when treasury bonds were traded in this network, the stocks listed on the securities exchanges in Shenzhen and Shanghai were brought in this net-work for trading.

Although many imperfections in or even absence of basic regulations and laws and material conditions remain, the Chinese capital market has developed remarkably in the space of a few years. The rapid accretion of securities and their trading volume on the capital market indicates that we can provide able indivi-duals with more scientific financial assets to meet their choice rather than the only traditional means of bank savings deposits. In the process of deepening financial reform and improving capital markets, however, attention must be paid to some key issues. New problems will still occur as the capital market contin-ues to grow. As to the mutual relations between the transactions on bonds and securities markets and the goals of more extensive economic policies, we need to analyze the major questions and respond to those of top priority.

2. Major Questions in the Development of China's Capital Market

Experts have pointed out that the major questions facing the further development of China's capital market can be summed up as follows:

(1) Environment of laws and regulations

Although nearly all fields in China's economic reform are restrained by the infrastructure, the effect of the backward telecommunications facilities on the development of unified capital market is especially severe. Market participants who first get access to existent infrastructural facilities are likely to take the opportunity for arbitrage. Regulations should be formulated to put an end to this conduct. In addition, rules and regulations should be enacted to reduce the delay in settlement and delivery, and see that all market participants are treated fairly and reasonably. Under the present conditions of serious shortage of infrastructural facilities in China, whether one can gain access to the market becomes all the more important.

A fierce challenge now confronting the Chinese government is how to create the necessary legal environment for the growth of capital market. To enable the stock market to achieve fully-fledged development, the question of ownership needs to be first solved in the relevant legislation for the capital market. Here, the contradiction between the publicly-acknowledged pressing need for the expansion of capital market and the principle of "public-ownership" in socialist countries arises. Despite the actual need for choosing the specific method of exercising ownership right in order to lessen the contradictions in the course of transforming state-owned enterprises to shareholding corporations, it is unimaginable to develop fully the capital market in China without the participation of state-owned enterprises which account for over 70 percent of the industrial fixed assets investment. Readjustments of industrial structure will be greatly promoted by introducing the input of more new capital through securitization of existing assets, thus giving more scope to guide the role of ownership by the people.

People find it hard to ascertain the nature of China's stock and the generally accepted international model cannot apply to Chinese enterprises because of the absence of corporation law and relevant commercial codes. Without such a legal basis, neither the securitization of assets nor the new-type collateral securities can be carried out. As the status of private investment in the capital structure of Chinese enterprises has yet to be defined, attempts to give a comprehensive and complete definition of the nature of Chinese enterprises have not been successful. There is no legal basis in the reform of state-owned enterprises and the extensive adoption of shareholding system. It is difficult for people to distinguish legally the distinct nature of the stocks of state-owned and private corporations, and reply to such questions as the negotiability of stock, and the right, obligation and investment risk of shareholders. It was once estimated that after the promulgation of Bankruptcy Law, an all-round system of corporation law would be quickly established; however, the development is not ideal. Some people also tried to define the nature of stocks listed on the securities exchanges in Shanghai and Shenzhen. In effect, the contents of the relevant laws and regulations of prevailing Sino-foreign joint ventures, based on which these stocks have been issued, are applied to China's domestic enterprises and become the legal basis for issuing stocks to the public.

The equity of shareholders needs to be defined and fully ensured in order to guarantee market transparency and fair treatment to all investors. The ownership of shareholders include the right of participation in operation and management, distribution of dividends, claim for capital in case of close-down or reorganization of corporations, the privilege enjoyed by the common stockholders in comparison with the holders of other stocks and securities, and the right of stockholders in stock transfer, taxation and other respects.

To formulate all-round rules of accounting and financial management and legalize them. Albeit the Chinese government has set about establishing an overall accounting system of internationally-recognized principles and practice, this work calls for a large amount of work and relevant legislation. Slow progress will delay the establishment and perfection of the whole system. In addition, subsequent to the introduction of the accounting system, efforts are needed to formulate and put into effect the accounting standards applicable to the departments concerned. Shanghai and Shenzhen Securities Exchanges published their respective provisional accounting standards governing the application for stock listing. The crux is that the lack of transparency in public accounting statements and auditor's reports of Chinese enterprises may weaken the confidence of the investors in the whole course. Over this, many foreign investors and brokers showed their concern time and again. The flotation of B shares with the face value in Renminbi was once foiled due to considerable difficulties around their issuance, which is not irrelevant to the standards of accounting and the principle of disclosure. In this respect, Shenzhen Securities Exchange, which was selected by the state as one of the first pilot units applying the new accounting standards, has gained marked results. This exchange is also benefited from the exemption of official commission for the initial flotation of stock by new companies.

The third major question in legislation is to set up one or several management organs which will support the public's confidence in the capital market on one hand, and supervise and ensure all parties abide by the relevant laws on the other. The adjustment here calls for discussing the relationship between self-discipline management and the management by the competent government departments. Even in Germany, a nation famous for its tradition of self-discipline, the general tendency is to employ the outside management of specialized agencies for ensuring the normal operation of the capital market. Detailed trading rules and standards for membership should be formulated concerning the stock exchange and the entire securities market, including curb markets and commodity exchanges (such as foreign exchange swap centers) to ensure fair and just transactions, the honesty of staff on the market and the trust and confidence by the public in capital market.

Drawing on the experience of Shenzhen Securities Exchange in handling the price fluctuations of stocks from mid-1990, and judging by the changes of the means of government intervention afterwards, the government has come to realize that more economic means should be employed in the management of stock market from a long-term point of view. Administrative means won't do. To bolster this viewpoint entails the establishment of a legal framework to get the market operating effectively. With the increase of the number of listed stocks on Shenzhen Securities Exchange, PE (price-earning) ratio plummeted from the peak level of 100:1 to the average of about 20:1. Government response to the fluctuations of stock prices is first to strengthen the administrative control; however, since ample funds on the market chased a small number of listed stocks, the government's effort has not dampened the enthusiasm of the investors. The establishment of a complete market managing system to protect the interests of investors and crack down on fraudulent trading will foster their confidence enormously. The principle of full disclosure will make the market operate more effectively on the basis of linking stock prices with the actual operational conditions of corporations; the market will not be driven by the excessive enthusiasm of speculators or affected by rigorous price control. Strict trading rules and codes of conduct should be worked out to make the market run effectively lest middlemen trade outside the market at prices divorced from that on the existing lawful market and thus create distorted market. The rules of over-the-counter trading are especially important to China. There are two reasons: First, with its vast territory and limited number of concentrated stock exchanges, China needs the establishment of a nationwide high-efficiency curb market system to ensure the access of investors to markets for their investments. Second, China's telecommunications facilities further restrict the growth of the securities market. Therefore, unless measures are adopted to safeguard this and more restrictive rules governing dealings on the stock exchanges and at the over-the-counter market nationwide are worked out, a small number of investors may use their prerogative to get advance information and gain unreasonable interests. As is seen above, to make sure the healthy development of market, the role of administrative organs is of vital importance.

What should be resolved is how to handle the relations between a unified nationwide market and the several scattered regional markets, and how to work out appropriate rules to unify the dispersed markets by permitting simultaneous transaction on different markets. In a sense, the Chinese government has set up more than two separate secondary markets. A question to be explained is that during the incipient developing stage of China's capital market, the ideal choice is to set up a unified market to guarantee the high liquidity. In a unified market comprising various transactions, high liquidity will bring enormous yields to both investors and securities issuers. High market liquidity may enlarge the volume of trade, reduce market fluctuations, ensure that investors conclude transactions with less cost at ideal prices, raise market operating efficiency, and eventually bring down the financing cost of issuers through decreasing the trading cost. As China has a vast territory, an effective medium has to be found to link various markets and to make them run in a uniform manner. Thus, arbitrage can be minimized, especially when government securities and public-owned shares form the main body of the capital market. On the other hand, the imbalance in China's regional economic growth also influences the need for establishing many regional exchanges connected with the effective telecommunications facilities and a system of settlement and delivery. What merits analysis is the experience in pit dealings and dealings of the curb market of the Securities Dealers' Automated Quotation System on the Shenzhen and Shanghai Securities Exchanges. Full consideration should also be given to the present shortage of infrastructural facilities and the future development of a telecommunications network so as to set up an effective market system. In the short term, it is necessary to take steps to further develop and perfect over-the-counter business in order to realize market unity and eliminate division in the market. In short, it is unlikely that a comprehensive legislative management system covering the formulation of corporation law and accounting law, and the establishment of management organs can be set up overnight. Provisional and special measures will have to be taken during the period to ensure the normal operation of the two securities exchanges and the observance of a code of conduct by member corporations and market participants. The adverse effect caused by fluctuations of stock prices on Shanghai and Shenzhen Securities Exchanges drew the intense concern of various quarters.

(2) Perfecting organization

Experts have pointed out that the second major aspect of the reform is the development and perfection of the relevant main organs. Both the market managing and supervising organs and the financial institutions participating in the market call for a specific course of development and a phased and steady growth. The crucial element for perfecting organs is the training of professional stock brokers, securities analysts and bond traders in the capital market. In the training course, consideration should be given to the re-training of accountants and related financial personnel according to internationally published principles and standards, thereby enabling them to meet the requirements of the new legislation in the near future. A main task of financial reform in the 1990s is to strengthen the building mechanism so as to promote the growth of capital market and perfect the financial system. One respect of the building mechanism is to make strict and definite stipulations on the establishment and abolishment of banks and non-banking financial institutions and ensure a competitive environment in financial services. Since state-owned specialized banks hold sway in China's financial system, earnest consideration should be given to whether they will be permitted to directly engage in the business of securities broking and underwriting.

The current settlement system is concentrated in the four large banks. Once small non-banking financial institutions have to counterbalance them directly, fair competition can not be ensured. Large banks are now setting up subsidiaries to conduct fresh financial business to meet the requirements of the existent regulations. Generally speaking, the development of numerous smaller financial institutions is of a significant bearing on further perfecting the capital market and the financial system. Some leading broking corporations and financial institutions from Hong Kong and other financial centers should be allowed to enter China's financial market in the form of solely-funded institutions or joint ventures with Chinese organizations. This will sharpen market competition, enlarge the scope of financial business and raise its level. In the formulation of the relevant management on the entry of foreign financial institutions into China's financial market, attention should be paid to the links of these foreign financial institutions with the Chinese existing enterprises and to the promotion of importing advanced management techniques and experience. To stimulate competition and prevent the four big banks from abusing power in their business due to their monopoly of the settlement system, an independent securities dealers' automated quotation system with incessant development and perfection is very important to raising the efficiency of the capital market.

(3) Structure of securities

The development of new financial instruments offers a chance for large-scale innovation in the capital market which is taking shape. Regarding how to implement a series of reform measures to help develop government securities market and the relevant money market, and how to ensure the government's effective management of debts and extensive use of indirect means and skills of monetary policy, many questions need to be studied and explored in practice. At present a project has been launched and put into effect involving technical assistant to financial and debt management departments. The series of measures include: to issue short-term securities (treasury bills and the bills of the People's Bank of China) to strengthen monetary management, to improve the method of floating medium- and long-term bonds on the primary market and gradually replace the rigid apportionments with underwriting, exclusive sales and auction, to develop and perfect the facilities and conditions at secondary market and over-the-counter transactions, to raise the standardization level and accuracy of forecasting on the primary market, to launch non-negotiable personal long-term savings securities, to develop open-market operations and to interfere in the secondary markets in an overall way.

(4) Market framework

According to the opinion of experts, the development sequence of various kinds of securities on China's stock market is not so distinct. It is partly attributed to the fact that enterprise reform has failed to go deeper and that there exist difficulties in the stock transfer of state-owned enterprises. The definition of ownership and assets appraisal of the existent enterprises encounter many technical and policy problems. The potential provided by the adjustment and reform of the enterprises exercises a much larger influence on the growth of securities market at least during the medium term than the effect of setting up new shareholding enterprises. However, the issuance of new securities during the reform of financial sectors is comparatively easy. Although the corporation law is to be promulgated, it is very easy to plan and issue new securities in the special Economic Zones of Shenzhen and Shanghai (Pudong) in accordance with the law on Chinese-foreign joint ventures. In spite of this, as stated above, the fundamental premise in this respect is that accounting and finance disclosure must be perfected. Only in this way can the interests of the investors be fully protected and the liquidity and transparency of the market be strengthened.

The reform sequence of government securities issuance is very definite. It includes the following points: To adopt such methods of issuances as underwriting, exclusive sales and auction so as to vary the structure of holders, to abolish the previous distribution method of compulsory administrative apportionment, and to enhance the government's ability to issue bonds at the lowest cost. As to the debenture and stock markets, priority must be given to perfecting the legislation and management system, and helping the necessary organs. Allowing experienced foreign investors to enter China's securities market will enormously strengthen and speed up the enhancement of issuing skills and the shift of the instruments at primary markets. During this process the linchpin is to remove the obstacles to entering the market and ensure the free inflow and outflow of capital while granting the tax credit.

(5) Restrictions of infrastructure

For the growth of secondary markets, it is necessary to perfect legislation for managing dealings, to encourage competition and protect the interests of investors. The most important step in the course of reform is to improve the infrastructural facilities relating to telecommunications, data collecting and processing, the banking business and the system of clearing and delivery in securities trading. As stated above, a major problem in this respect is whether China should develop a sequence of scattered primary and secondary markets, which are mutually connected, and also connected with the various over-the-counter transactions centres through telecommunications system. The decision on the development of Shenzhen and Shanghai markets gave rise to a problem, namely, whether to envisage the further tapping of new market centres or, as the next step, to focus the energy on raising the efficiency of the two markets formed and to build up a unified market via telecommunications trading in some over-the-counter transaction centres. Even if telecommunications facilities and a computerized trading system develop very rapidly, because of China's vast territory and numerous enterprises, it remains feasible to build up scattered markets connected by telecommunications. The market can further develop only following the completion of the planned basic legislation, organizations and material facilities.

The restriction of infrastructure is no doubt the most serious obstacle to the development of a unified market, the expanded market liquidity and the reinforced competition. Obviously, a nationwide clearance and delivery system should be first set up to protect the interests of both investors and securities dealers. The prevailing clearing and delivery system obviously suits neither the need for the growth of modern stock and bond markets nor that for strengthening the liquidity and transparency of dealings. The implementation of the telecommunications development plan will make the nation's most important commercial hubs realize partial unification, and extend telecommunications to the main cities and townships at the turn of this century. In spite of improved telecommunications, it will still take a long time to improve customer-oriented services unless the government adopts every possible measure to develop dynamically users' network and telecommunications services, including the development of users' groups and significant customers. The capital market should develop in harmony with state telecommunications policy to iron out inconsistency and incompatibility. Otherwise, the cost of unifying capital market will be increased and the introduction of advanced technology in this field hampered.

3. Steps for the Reform of the Capital Market

(1) To foster the stock market continuously. Some experts hold that China's stock market has taken initial shape. Restricted by the factor of ownership, its development has confronted many problems. State-owned stocks cannot be negotiated and transferred on the market while the stock owned by legitimate persons can only be traded among enterprises of legitimate persons, which has limited to a great extent the expansion and development of the stock markets. At present many transformed shareholding enterprises are eager to list their stocks on the exchanges, but overlook the management of their enterprises within the principles of shareholding. Consequently the crux of the development of the stock market rests on the healthy growth of the shareholding economy. What should be done now is to advance actively the reform of pilot shareholding enterprises, to adhere to the policy of the transition from flotation with fixed direction to public flotation and to go through rigorous examination and approval formalities of listing. Another nationwide stock exchange should be quickly set up in an economic centre in the north to form the framework of a national stock market system. Regional stock exchanges will be set up in economically-developed regions in due course. Information quotations should be perfected, the delivery and clearing system reinforced, and rules of market dealings and competition improved so as to realize open, fair and just transac-

tions on the market.

(2) To tap long-term bond market. The development of the market of medium- and long-term bonds in the capital market should include the following two factors: first, the transformation of operating mechanism of the enterprise; second, the progress of enterprise-like reform of the bank. Only when the development of the long-term bond market synchronizes with these two factors, can the credit inflation be avoided that is caused by the blind flotation of bonds and by excessive bank lending. While reliably increasing the variety and issuing amount of bonds, it is necessary to adhere to the principle of linking interest rate with the credit rating of bonds, the interest to keep a reasonable structure of interest rates by adjusting the interest rate level of bonds, to set up and improve the systems of bonds redemption, of guarantee for issued bonds, and of sinking funds, to improve the method of selling bonds, accelerate the development of secondary markets of bonds, and ensure the negotiation, transfer and encashment of bonds. All this will help the healthy growth of the primary bond market.

(3) To accelerate the perfection of the treasury bonds market. In the development of the bonds market, a strong treasury bonds market boosts the growth of the entire bonds market. This is an important international experience. At present the Chinese market should be improved in the following respects: first, increase the frequency of issuing treasury bonds, changing the annual concentrated issue into several issues a year; secondly, diversify the redemption time of treasury bonds (such as to issue treasury bills to make up deficits of annual fiscal expenditures); thirdly, adopt flexible and varying methods of subscription and underwriting; fourthly, substitute the floating interest rate for that of fixed coupon rates; fifthly, allow enterprises to enter markets for dealings and restore the overall functions of market.

(4) To perfect organization and management systems of the securities market. One more important aspect in the building and development of securities market is the organization and management systems of the market. Various securities laws and regulations should be perfected and a securities appraisal mechanism

formed. In the light of China's current conditions and the characteristics of her financial industry, by no means should the growth of securities market precede its programming. Development should go hand in hand with programming or programming before development. Securities law and securities transaction law should be enacted in light of the actual conditions of China and in reference to international practice, thus providing laws governing the operation and control of financial market.

(5) To further develop and perfect non-bank financial institutions. Considerable non-bank financial institutions (such as corporations of financial leasing, securities, trust, credit standing appraisal, investment fund management, enterprise group finance, and insurance) have been successively formed and developed in keeping with the advance of financial industry. Positive support should be given to these corporations for their perfection and rapid development. Urban credit cooperatives should be developed actively, and in the areas where conditions are available, some pilot urban co-operative banks consisting of urban credit co-operatives may be formed in the service of individually run urban businesses and petty collective enterprises. To tap the resources of financial markets, effort should be made to let various social funds participate in the activities of financial markets. The funds may include the trade union fund, pension fund, medical insurance fund, children welfare fund, relief fund, education fund, religion fund, and funds of famous persons. The development and perfection of financial institutions means a brisk and prosperous capital market.

4. How to Manage and Develop Non-bank Financial Institutions

China's non-bank financial institutions have developed very rapidly, but should be subject to strengthened management to ensure their growth.

A question facing China in the 1980s was how to manage these institutions and promote their development, for they played an indispensable role or even became the underlying sectors in the development of the financial market.

Non-bank institutions have played an important part in the financial system, though they do not take in deposits. Over recent years, hundreds of such institutions have been formed in China, mainly as trust and investment corporations. Chinese insurance companies have also expanded very fast over the past few years. However, the recent management has imposed certain limitations on the development of insurance companies, restricting them to enter the Chinese financial market. The question to be encountered by China in a few years ahead will be how to develop institutional investors. They include insurance companies, pension funds, trust and investment corporations and investment funds, and will be primary institutions in the development of China's securities industry in the future. The investment funds founded by some of the above organizations will play a great role in deepening the financial market. With a view to creating an environment for the development of these institutions, management should be further bettered, systems improved and laws perfected, especially the enactment of the legal system for their entry into and exit from the financial market, and the betterment of accounting and settlement system.

These institutions can build a bridge between individual investors and corporations likely to be listed and offer some instruments of investment. Judging the situation in China, it is crucial to make these institutions the intermediary of investment. They can also become the intermediary of banks. People can deposit their savings in the non-bank financial institutions. Therefore, these institutions can become organizations pooling funds for the financial market, particularly individual funds because they can transfer the savings to the financial market. Based on this, a large number of non-bank financial institutions now exist in China. The next step is to support and lend technical assistance to them and to promote their development and raise their all-around abilities through cooperation and joint ventures with their foreign counterparts. On one hand, it is necessary to develop capital markets and increase listed corporations; on the other, it is very important to further develop intermediate institutions, particularly those serving individual investors, and this perhaps is more fundamental.

5. China's Urgent Need: Building a Modernized Banking System

In the opinion of some experts, the present reform of China's financial system should focus on establishing a modernized banking system rather than developing a capital market.

This does not mean that the above two goals are contradictory. They are mutually co-ordinate and complement in function, rather than being mutually replaceable. Of course, ideally there should be overall financial system reform and improvements in every sector.

Given the limited resources, financial resources in particular, several priority strategies should be formulated. First priority in financial reform should be to set up a modernized banking system rather than a capital market. Below are the major reasons:

In the incipient stage of capital accumulation, bank deposits are a fairly good object of investment compared with other financial assets. As far as a capital supplier is concerned, the bank deposit is a proper investment tool with relatively better earnings and less risks: As to the allocation of funds, it is more beneficial to invest funds in promising enterprises with better performance through the banking system. Through financing by banks, long-term face-to-face relations can be established between fund demander and fund supplier, and between borrower and bank.

That China is a country with a vast territory inevitably calls for a comparatively decentralized structure. A capital market itself entails highly centralized information. During the budding stage of growth, it is perhaps less suitable for China to give prior development to the capital market.

Certain experts emphasize the diversification of financial intermediate institutions, holding that the burden of fund-raising in China which should have been borne by public sectors has now been shifted onto banks in the form of bank loans, and that the burden would be better returned to the public sector. Other experts disagree, holding that the most striking question in China at present is the setting up of a modernized banking system instead of diversifying financial intermediate institutions. According to them, the set-up of this system is the pressing priority in China, while the management of the capital market does not head the agenda in terms of China's present conditions. The modernized banking system is a competitive banking system, that is, one in which banks operate on their own at their own risk. This competition is vitally important to current conditions of China.

Non-bank savings institutions are not new either in Taiwan or on China's mainland. They existed nationwide before the Anti-Japanese War but subsequently disappeared because of inflation. Stable currency is the basic condition for their existence. After the currency was stabilized in Taiwan, non-bank institutions such as insurance companies and savings cooperatives swiftly reappeared. However, there is quite inadequate management of the non-bank savings institutions. New laws have been enacted and put into effect, but are not carried out to the letter. Although such institutions are called non-bank institutions, the government hopes that they can share risks like banks. Only in so doing can they protect the interests of depositors. We should therefore have very strict regulations restricting them from focusing their investments on one and the same aspect such as buying the same asset or lending to one or a few persons. Non-bank saving institutions should be regarded as banks and awarded the function of sharing investment risks.

Unlike common banks, non-bank institutions may engage in the medium- and long-term investment. The most important thing is that the central bank has a system of stable money supply by which non-bank savings institutions can make medium- and long-term lending and absorb deposits in terms of the units of currency. In the absence of a stable currency, how will they enter into contracts with insurance companies? For instance, who will insure his life in case of an unstable currency? Therefore, the first premise on which non-bank institutions exist is a stable currency. The second premise is the strict implementation of their regulating so that they will not be manipulated by one enterprise or invest in one asset.

Chapter V
Monetary Policy

The basic goal of the economic policy of any government is to promote sustained growth under the condition of price stability. From this perspective, development and efficiency in the financial sector is vital. Financial policy and the organizational set-up determine the pooling of savings, the use and investment performance of which directly affect economic growth.

Reform of the financial market is of primary importance in ensuring stability in the countries undergoing structural readjustment and economic restructuring at the same time. Now people realize that these two measures are interrelated and complement each other; especially financial reform which plays a crucial role in effective structural readjustment. The most important objective of financial reform is to free the financial system so as to raise its efficiency and steadiness, thus sharpening competition by letting the market mechanism play its role freely. Financial reform revolves around three main aspects: improving the monetary control system in keeping with the development of the monetary market; reform in the supervision and cautious management system; to set up or develop various kinds of new-type financial institutions and financial intermediates, to sharpen the competition among banks (for instance, to loosen the restrictions on entering the banking system), and to develop a long-term capital market.

International experience shows that the various measures of financial reform do not have a sole or an optimal sequence. However, experience also indicates that these measures must be extensive and comprehensive to ensure the effectiveness of reform (or to shorten the transition stage when there inevitably exist elements affecting the stability). Especially when introducing "basic factors" of the market, it is necessary to conduct a crucial package of reforms involving many departments at the same time. According to similar international experience, the absence of measures ensuring stability and the relevant supporting reforms in financial departments may lead to greater instability. The fiscal imbalance should be put forward firmly from the onset of the process of reform. An important aspect of fiscal reform involves the development of various substitutive sources of revenue and the repeal of inflationary taxes and other discriminative taxes levied on financial departments, such as borrowings from the banking system by means of unnecessary high reserves and liquidity requirements which reduce bank profits. Adequate control of the money supply is necessary for the creation of a steady macro-economic environment. International experience indicates that during the process of structural readjustment, the carrying out of reform in money control at the very beginning can bring about marked advantages.

The shift from direct control to indirect one can best improve monetary control. Direct control is highly complex. Under general circumstances, after a period of time (for instance, in China) it will lose efficacy when the evading motive leads to the formation of informal or unlawful inter-enterprise borrowing markets. Direct control such as credit upper limit, and credit and interest rate limits of banks or departments weakens the efficiency of financial intermediates and also of resources allocation.

1. China's Monetary Policy: Current Situation and Questions

In the opinion of some experts, the macro monetary policy centring on credit planning is out of step with market economy.

The credit plan put into effect as from 1988 is a tripartite planning model composed of loan incremental scale, deposit plan and cash issuing plan. From the process of preparing and implementing the plan, the deposit plan and the cash issuing plan are beyond the control of the central bank, while the loan scale is compulsorily implemented by administrative measures. The latter neither had the basis of scientific theory and method nor can reflect the demand for the real economic function.

The gap between the results implementing monetary policy and the expected plan in China is by far the biggest, compared with those of central banks in other countries worldwide. The biggest difference amounted to 2.35 folds and the lowest one of 17 percent, all being positive figures. The plan of the loan scale was adjusted even in early December in some years. The positive or negative gap between the scheduled plan and its actual implementation is also quite big in the input of cash. .

Facts reveal that China will get nowhere if its prospective monetary policy follows the beaten path centring on the credit plan. Owing to unforeseeable market demand and the impact of multiple aspects in the economic activities of enterprises and individuals, and owing to the market-oriented trend of macroeconomic variables such as price, savings, investment and sales, the prepared credit plan is unable to foresee accurately the moving loci of the above variables. On the other hand, the activities of economic entities cannot be restricted by the credit plan. The most convincing proof is that previous credit plans were all based on the growth rate of a planned economy, the margin of planned price increase and the unchanged interest rate, while actually the changes in China's economic structure have long since made the several big variables move beyond the control of the plan. The plan of the credit scale, for instance, was set at 170 billion yuan in early 1990, based on the GNP growth rate of 8 percent and the retail price growth rate of 10 percent. The credit plan was allegedly framed according to "scientific projection" and was not to be exceeded. In the event, the three readjustments of credit scale raised the figure to 270 billion yuan mid-year and the actual year-end amount was 273.1 billion yuan. The real GNP growth rate was 5.2 percent and price rise rate only 2.1 percent that year.

Consequently experts proposed that China's monetary policy in the 1990s should not frequently readjust the credit plan, but should abandon the plan altogether. It was proposed the policy completely abolish control of credit scale and give up planned control of direct financing increments (the amount of issued bonds and stocks). The substitution is the monetary policy with the growth margin of money supply as the intermediate target.

The instability and imbalance of macro-economy that occurred in China in the latter half of the 1980s was mainly caused by the absence of strict discipline of monetary policy.

Many analysts in China and abroad attribute the lack of monetary discipline to the drawback of policies, that is, during the process of implementing the strategy of high-paced growth in the mid-1980s, the government lacked sufficient commitment to control currency and credit aggregates. However, this explanation seems too oversimplified, it probably covers part of more important facts while speaking about other aspects of them.

China's leaders perhaps underestimated the danger of inflation in the mid-1980s, and today the government is certainly working at price stability. However, the government has to adopt an easy monetary policy and stimulate the economy anew by sustained and large input of credit. Investment and industrial output once again reached worryingly high levels. At the same time new problems appear, that is, a tight monetary policy may have to be adopted due to another round of inflationary pressure. The "stop-and-go" model of the actual operation of the Chinese economy and the drawing up of its policy makes people ask: Whether the current organizational setup and control mechanism of China's financial system can provide the government with a suitable monetary weapon for achieving effective macroeconomic control.

1) Structural Restrictions on Policy Formulation

A question at issue is that structural drawbacks have limited the government's ability to launch any kind of monetary policy which can both boost economic growth and maintain financial stability. Structural factors, especially the lack of a suitable organization and controlling instruments to fine tune the economy in an established system of policy present the government with a difficult choice between the two extremes of monetary policy. It may either adopt a relaxed monetary policy to boost economic growth, which will give rise to the danger of inflation, or use the relative tight monetary policy which will lead to economic decline. If a government lacks an organization or instrument to fine tune its economy in an established or chosen system of policy, it will be obliged to manage its economy mainly by means of momentous changes, including those in the policy system. This is the case, for example, of fast economic growth in the periods 1981-1984 and 1986-1988, and of austerity in early 1985 and the 1988-1990 period. It must be admitted that the complex model of China's monetary and economic policies perhaps may be overstated to some extent, however, we hold that this is the sole reasonable explanation of the questions below, that is, why does China swing between the too relaxed and the too tight monetary policies and why is China's economic movement always in periodic "stop-and-go" cycles?

Experts hold that the basic problem of China's effective monetary management is that the changes of the monetary policy in goals, measures and instruments have generally lagged behind those of economic structure.

Before the reform, pricing and money in the Chinese economy basically played a passive role in the allocation of resources in direct and compulsory industrial planning systems. They were the main tools of direct control and accounting, the output and investment plans worked out by the planning departments were undertaken and controlled by unified fund distribution which was carried out in the light of the state's cash and credit plans. Monetary policy is mainly for realizing the targets of the real economy, particularly for distributing funds to pre-decided departments of priority. Furthermore, it is merely one of the numerous direct control mediums (among which, the unified distribution plan of input in kind is perhaps most important in the system of distribution in kind), while the weak point of monetary control may be remedied through more rigorous control on distribution in kind.

However, with the momentous changes in the structure and setup of China's economy brought about by the market-oriented economic reform as started in 1987, money and credit have come the most important and most principal instruments in indirect macro-economic management. In the meantime, these changes have also indicated that the previous method and targets of monetary control are superfluous, or are against productive forces. To give an example; although the monetary policy is now regarded as a tool of indirect control, its control on monetary credit and other financial variables remains chiefly direct. Therefore, the position of monetary policy is becoming more important daily in China's macro-control, nevertheless, its functioning method and effect cannot meet the requirements of economic restructuring. Monetary policy has shown some worrying characteristics: The policy tended to be less strict and too lenient towards excessive investment, overheated economy and inflationary pressure. Response to and revision of the policy were sometimes slow and late. At other times, it swayed between the two extremes over a very short span, leading to widespread fund problems and dramatic economic fluctuations. Moreover, the tight anti-inflationary policy was often relaxed too early for fear that continuation would retard the economy, and consequently the monetary policy seemed to become "hostage" to the unreasonable system.

Given the present setup, the economic policy is not purposeful but responsive, responding to events instead of taking the initiative to control them. The new system in which the monetary policy operates has two main trends or features: The first is the fast and extensive monetization of the economy. During the 1979-1988 period, the aggregate savings in state banks grew by an average of 20.7 percent a year and per-capita savings went up by 33.7 percent. The financial system has replaced the budget to become the most important source of investment and working capital.

Another more significant feature is: with the enormous weakening of the priority power in controlling resources by the state and the central government, reform in administrative decentralization and market orientation has notably changed the relative importance and functions of various economic departments and organs in the economy. Besides the narrowed scope of the compulsory plan, the following are important to the new overall design of the methods and tools of macro-economic control, particularly to monetary and financial policies.

(1) The importance and role of households in the economy have been strengthened. During the 1979-1987 period, their average annual savings deposits in state banks went up by 26.7 percent from 40.6 to 269 billion yuan. Of the total savings deposits of the state, the share of households increased from 24 percent in 1979 to 66 percent in 1989; of the national income (net material products) the estimated household share rose from about 57 percent in 1987 to 70 percent in 1989. During the same period, the proportion of the bank deposits of households shot from 7 percent to 38 percent of the national income. Nowadays, China's households have replaced the state in becoming the most important component of savings in the economy.

(2) The expanding share of non-state sectors on the market. Of the industrial output value, the share held by state-owned enterprises dropped from 78 percent in 1987 to 56 percent in 1989, and the state-owned ratio in the sectors of construction, transportation and commerce (retails) stood at 31 percent and less than 50 percent in 1989. In those important means of production still distributed by the state, the share distributed by the market was increased to 49 percent in coal, 60 percent in timber, 78 percent in metal plates and 88 percent in power generation equipment. The state share in the industrial output value is only 56 percent at present. In view of the fact that the industrial share accounts for only 40 percent of the GDP, the proportion of state-owned sectors in China's economy only reached 35 percent of the GDP, a proportion slightly higher than those of many Western countries practising market economy in the early 1980s such as Britain and Italy.

(3) The weakened control by the central authorities (the state) over resources. The share of government revenue in the national income has declined considerably since 1987. During the 1987-1988 period, the proportion of revenue in the national income fell from 37.2 percent to a mere 19 percent. In 1979, 75

percent of the capital construction investment of the state sectors came from the budget, but in 1988 the figure went down to 25 percent. In the same period, the amount of non-budgetary or outside-budgetary funds (the portion distributed by local governments, departments and enterprises) grew from an equivalent of 31 percent to 94.8 percent compared with the fiscal revenue. In other words, about 50 percent of the financial resources (excluding those belonging to households) in the economy have now drifted away from direct budgetary control.

2) Monetary Policy as a Restraining Policy

The changes of the relative importance and functions of the different bodies and sectors, especially the decentralization control of resources, have pushed forward and promoted the huge investment expansion of the central ministries, localities and enterprises enormously. The root of the structural "hunger for investment" is a combination of the shortcomings of both the state-owned enterprise system and the fiscal system. As the ongoing reform of enterprises has not resolved the problem of soft budgetary restraints, this phenomenon encourages enterprises to seek the maximum development of their production capacity regardless of efficiency. The current financial system of separating central from local revenue (especially the system for contracted responsibility) has induced local governments (and ministries) to help stimulate the enterprises within their jurisdiction to enlarge their investment and production. For the purposes of hitting the contracted targets of fiscal turn-over to the central government and obtaining the maximum amount of funds for their localities, local governments will serve their own interests at best through enlarging the production scale of local enterprises and expanding the other economic activities which may increase income.

In the state-owned enterprises, and in the fiscal relationship between the management authorities and enterprises, or between central and local governments, the only mechanism to stimulate interest is to encourage investment. It is against this background that the question of China's monetary policy has been put forward. This background may be further explained to be the partial reform in economic restructuring and the structural preference and demand for large-scale investment of both enterprises and localities.

In essence, the monetary policy is a restraining one, and it is difficult to carry out in any country because it involves difficult alternative and economic choices. The objective of monetary policy is to restrict or limit the availability of funds so as to be consistent with the actual amount needed economically under the conditions of not breaking price stability and economic balance as a whole. The monetary policy as a restraining one is all the more pressing in China.

The reasons for this urgency are: First, as stated above, the demand for funds is very big and strong from the start due to the problems of structure. Second, China has launched an ambitious growth plan which needs a large amount of investment. Therefore, any restraining monetary policy is very easily regarded erroneously or censured as being inconsistent with the overall developing objective. Politically it is very easy to adopt a supporting monetary policy instead of a restraining one. Third, Chinese state-owned enterprises are not only organizations of production, they are "miniature societies" in charge of a series of duties which should be borne by society. Any tight monetary policy restricting the production and investment activities of enterprises naturally leads to unacceptable social consequences. Fourth, the drawbacks of the fiscal system have to be remedied by the financial system. To reduce the visible scale of fiscal deficit, it is necessary to make sizable fiscal overdraft and policy-oriented loans through the banking system. This not only contravenes the commercial principle that the big four specialized banks should follow in their operation, but also brings about serious difficulties in the government's control of monetary and credit aggregates.

The four features indicate that the restraining monetary policy is very difficult to carry in China. Nevertheless, the above features also strongly indicate that in order to maintain economic stability, China must adopt a restraining monetary policy.

However, if China adopts such a monetary policy, the part of the central bank's current functions in contradiction with macro-control should be assigned to other departments in the financial system. Especially, it is unsuitable for the monetary policy to take care of specific business such as directly distributing funds. And these functions are better left to commercial banks and other types of financial intermediaries. At present, excessive dependence on monetary policy and banking systems to fulfil the government's various development targets has not produced any real effective monetary policy that can be implemented.

If the effectiveness of China's monetary policy is raised, two interrelated measures must be adopted: firstly, to rearrange the organs of the system of the central bank and monetary control so as to make them capable of resisting pressure from all sectors asking for support of their economic expansion; secondly, to develop the capital market and make the most efficient use of capital. The second measure is an important premise of the first. For example, if the purpose is to shift to the complex indirect means of monetary control such as open market operations by the monetary authorities, the premise is the existence of a developed capital market. Meanwhile as large amounts of securities and financial instruments appear with the development of the capital market, the monetary control authorities may have more means to adjust and control the funds available to the financial intermediates.

Foreign experts hold that the question of China's monetary policy lies in the following: historically, whenever decentralization invests the power to decide production and investment to local governments, there will always touch off a strong impulse towards investment expansion. This impulse has become much stronger since 1978 because decentralization is very different from the past in both extent and in its nature (market operation). Changes have taken place in the channels of monetary control. The main function of distributing funds has changed from fiscal sectors to banks. On the whole, however, reform has been only partially effected and the logic and operating features of the old economic structure (strong thirst for investment and the irrational use of resources) still exist.

A very effective mechanism has been provided for ministries of the central government, local governments and enterprises by the previous administrative structure, and through this mechanism the pressure caused by their demand for funds can be transmitted to the monetary authorities. However, the central bank of China lacks the authority to withstand pressure from interference with support for expansion. Under the circumstances, the government and the central bank have to resort to direct monetary control. This control brings losses to the efficiency of allocation in spite of the short-term benefit, and deals bigger blows to supply rather than to demand, thus aggravating the economic imbalance. China's monetary controlling channels may have changed but the controlling methods and mechanism have basically remained. Even if these are not counterproductive, these are outdated and inefficient at least.

3) Drawbacks of Dual Objective of Monetary Policy: Aggravating Economic Fluctuations and Hampering Optimized Resources Allocation

The monetary policy of China has proceeded with difficulty for years under the dual objectives of economic growth and currency stabilization, and sometimes it will also bear the functions of readjusting industrial structure. This results from the influence of the structure of planned distribution which directly distributes part of bank credit as material resources and is inconsistent with the principle of allocating resources based on the law of value in the structure of market economy. With the transition of the Chinese economic structure toward that of market economy, direct distribution of social resources by the government will be gradually reduced, and price will be decided more and more by market supply and demand. Under the structure of market economy, the control of aggregate social demand and that of total pricing levels to a great extent will depend on the control of money supply. To maintain steady economic growth, the objective of monetary policy of the central bank shall make a gradual transition to the unitary objective—currency stabilization.

In the opinion of some experts, monetary policy with economic growth as its objective will aggravate economic fluctuations.

After 15 years of economic restructuring, the development and operation of China's economy have gradually deepened and have a greater dependence on finance, and the influence of the changes in total money supply on the economy has become increasingly clear. China's economy grew at high speed due to the marked increase of money supply M_1 in 1984, 1988 and 1992, while negative economic growth occurred in the first quarters of 1986 and 1989 owing to the short supply of M_1 in the previous years and this even adversely affected the economic growth through the whole year. When the banking industry is highly monopolized, credit control chiefly depends on administrative means and enterprises excessively rely on bank credit for their funds, it is difficult to fix the quantity when the policy of money aggregate is used to stimulate the economy. This policy might give rise to big economic fluctuations.

Controlling credit mainly by administrative means is difficult to curb both the total credit and the structure of money supply, causing big fluctuations of money supply. China's financial industry is a highly monopolized one. In terms of total balance at the end of 1992, 92 percent of the exogenous financing of non-financial sectors came from the loans of financial institutions, and 71 percent of the total loans were granted by the four big specialized banks. As the four big banks that are in charge of the important policy and commercial functions fail to form the mechanism of self restraint and the situation of equal competition, they often force the central bank to supply an excessive amount of base currency. Confronted with excess base currency, the central bank has to limit the expansion of credit by assigning loan quotas. The quotas are often forced to be adjusted under the pressure of conflicts of interests among the grassroots branches of specialized banks and even the central bank. The range of the quota adjustments has exceeded 30 percent since 1989. The gap between the growth of credit scale and that of money supply has increased continuously, so has been its effect on economic fluctuations.

Generally speaking, the enlargement of any total social demand with payment ability is basically decided by the growth of broad money supply which is M_2 in China. Loans are not direct purchasing power, and only after the enterprises (organizations or individuals) translate them into deposits or cash can they make purchases directly or by check. To explore the degree of influence on total demand by the control of loan scale, the comparative analysis between the increment of loans and that of money supply M_2 may provide a basic conclusion. A comparison of the annual increment of M_2 (state banks and rural credit cooperatives) and that of loans in China in the period 1983-1992 is shown in the following table.

Annual Increases of Money Supply M_2 and Loans in the Period 1983-1992

(unit = 100 million yuan)

Year	1983	1984	1985	1986	1987	1988	1989	1990	1991	1992
M_2 Increase	520	1250	756	1522	1665	1711	1856	3312	4088	6050
Loan Increase	646	1352	1183	1845	1650	1679	2011	3085	3269	4228
Annual difference	-126	-102	-427	-323	15	32	-155	227	819	1822

As indicated in the table above, the loan scale was basically bigger than M_2 or both were equal before 1990, in other words, the control of loan scale was basically efficacious in regulating the total social demand during the period. The gap between M_2 and loan scale rapidly grew after 1990. M_2 exceeded the loan increase 43.1 percent in 1992 and the loan quota was by and large ineffective in regulating the total social demand. This shows the unavoidable influence on planned control by the development of market economy. The basic causes can be summed up in three points: The development of financial markets, the diversification of financial instruments, and the establishment of priority status of interests in specialized banks and other financial institutions.

The excessive dependence on banks for enterprise capital gives no buffer zone to the implementation of monetary policy and may directly lead to economic fluctuations. The proportion of the capital owned by China's enterprises, state-owned enterprises in particular, is decreasing year by year. Before economic restructuring, the investment in fixed assets of the state-owned enterprises was generally provided by the state, and 52 percent of their working capital were supplied by themselves. In 1992, 40 percent of their investment in fixed assets and 80 percent of their working capital came from bank loans. China's capital market has grown to a certain extent in recent years, but it occupies only a very small share (8 percent) of the total social credit. The high proportion of enterprises' exogenous financing comes mainly from bank credit. When banks adopt a tight money policy, enterprises suffer from direct and strong shock because they have no other alternatives of financing. In this mechanism, monetary policy seems to affect directly the economic growth, but actually it can neither effectively control the total money supply nor leave some leeway. Hence the resultant aggravation of economic fluctuations.

According to some financial experts, the dual objectives of monetary policy cannot promote the optimized allocation of resources.

A tight or relaxed monetary policy cannot automatically regulate resources allocation in the market economy. The allocation of social resources is mainly the result of the law of value and the law of equalized profit rate, but the policy of total money supply cannot directly influence the allocation. The amount of money supply may affect the level of market interest rate, and further the demand of enterprise for credit. Given the level of certain interest rate (cost of capital), however, fund allocation is decided by the prices of commodity supply and demand. Economic growth is not measured by the total input and its more important factor is the increase efficiency of resources utilization. The latter needs a stable standard of value to measure the various resources and a price system to compare input and output, this is related to the stability of currency value.

Under the structure that the government bears responsibility for economic growth and manages the economy directly, the dual objective of monetary policy tends to aggravate the tendency of chasing economic growth while overlooking the stability of currency.

It is common to governments worldwide to bear responsibility for economic growth. To achieve this objective, governments running market economies tend to establish an environment of equal competition and maintain good economic order. Therefore, they attach more importance to building a legal system and structural innovation, and since the result of economic activity and the ultimate responsibility are dispersed, there is no pressure of directly interfering in finance. In such a country of structural transition as China, in which market order and regulations on competition are being established, its government is often chiefly responsible for the consequences of economic activities. When economic contradictions become intensified, it will choose the approach of direct interference in finance to delay the outbreak of contradictions.

The biggest problem facing China's economy, for instance, is low economic results. China has relatively limited resources in the light of its huge population, and so a serious problem confronting its development is how to use effectively the existing resources. To raise efficiency means to sift out some enterprises with low economic results, but the ensuing problem of employment prevents the government from resolutely carrying out structural readjustment. It cannot help but use an expanding credit policy to conceal this situation, that is, to give profit-making enterprises some money to maintain economic growth and also to give loss-making enterprises some money in exchange of temporary stability. The result: Inflationary pressure increases and resources allocation can hardly be optimized.

4) Measures of Reinforcing the Discipline of Monetary Policy

Experts are of the opinion that there are some conspicuous features in China's economic, political and administrative structures, namely, the pressure calling for monetary policy to support economic expansion is very strong and the pressure can be conveyed effectively to the policy makers of the central authorities. If it is admitted that the monetary policy should be a restraining one, the setup and restraining method will have to be designed anew so as to let the monetary authorities face the heavy pressure to formulate and carry out such a policy.

Like many other countries carrying out financial reform, more and more Chinese have turned their attention to the independence of the central bank in recent years, regarding it as a way of ensuring the discipline of monetary policy. For a better discipline of monetary policy, in fact, the independence of the central bank is only a necessary condition but not a sufficient one. There exists another danger, that is, the independence of the central bank is regarded as a panacea for solving the highly sophisticated monetary and financial problems in China. And these problems, just as discussed above, are caused by a series of interrelated structural and political elements.

However, the viewpoint of the independence of the central bank is conducive to focusing attention on the related problems which need to be posed and solved.

(1) Experts have pointed out that China's monetary policy should have a definite objective: price stability.

Some questions need to be discussed and clarified, such as the objective of monetary policy in its narrow sense. What has given us a very deep impression is that China's monetary policy includes extensive contents. Of them the most important basic contents are two, namely, price stability and economic growth (like employment, industries and structural adjustment). The two basic objectives can be consistent and mutually strengthened in certain special cases or in a very short span of time, but they are often antagonistic to each other. In order to keep pricing stable, the monetary authorities strive to control the money supply. On the other hand the authorities become the supplier of funds to achieve the objective of economic growth. Can the central bank at once perform the two functions at the same time?

Both international and China's own experience (in modern times with the great leap forward of 1950s and the small leap forward of the 1970s) all indicated that when monetary authorities strived to fulfil the objectives of economic growth and employment, price instability is inevitable. Moreover, sufficient proof has shown that money has an asymmetrical impact on price and economy and that it can forcibly control inflationary pressure but avails little to stimulate the growth of output and employment in the medium- and long-run. From this point of view, the goal of monetary policy should be what it can best do: to create an environment of stable pricing which maintains sustained economic growth and leaves the objective of economic growth to fiscal and other policy instruments. Only under this environment can commercial banks and non-bank financial institutions function as direct suppliers of funds.

Without reconsidering the basic functions and objectives of monetary policy and the central bank, a fresh design of China's monetary system will not better the discipline of monetary policy. China's monetary policy entails a clear, definite and unitary objective, that is, price stability. At present, like many of China's state-owned enterprises, they seemingly serve too many masters but in fact none at all. China's monetary policy serves too many objectives, but actually serves none of them.

(2) In the opinion of experts, China calls for unitary management authorities which formulate and put into effect monetary policy on their own.

People often comment: It is not the People's Bank of China but the State Council that decides the monetary policy. In principle, it does not affect the overall situation whoever formulates the policy as long as it is correct. Yet there is one vital point, namely, the relevant authorities that ultimately shape the monetary policy must be separated and freed from the strong economic and political pressure calling for the support of economic expansion. However, like the cabinets of other countries, one of the functions of the State Council is to understand and coordinate the interests of governmental sectors and local governments. Furthermore, the State Council is responsible for more extensive developmental objectives which constantly conflict with the goal of price stability. Like other countries, the central government is vulnerable to the influences of demand from its component agencies, ministries and local governments. In this case, essentially it is not the cabinet or government but the ministries of the central government, local governments and state-owned enterprises that decide upon the monetary policy.

From the above, the argument is very simple; whoever decides the monetary policy must withstand the pressure of expansion. The economic management work of the State Council will become easier if such an agency subordinate to the government as the central bank formulates the monetary policy together with the authorities. This is because a subordinating agency of the government, serving as a buffer body of the State Council, may bear the pressure from ministries and local governments. The above two principles are two aspects of the same question: that is, many objectives of monetary policy derive from the influences exercised by many policy makers or many groups of vested interests in the framing of monetary policy, and vice versa. If there is only one definite and unitary chief objective in the monetary policy, it is very easy to reduce the number of policy makers in the course of formulating the monetary policy. Moreover, this may decrease the possibility and scope of interference. On the contrary, the premise of formulating the monetary policy by unitary management authorities is to have a strictly-defined objective of monetary policy.

(3) Low fiscal interference within the monetary system

In the opinion of experts, the concept of the independence of the central bank is roughly outlined and is indeed hard to quantify. One of its meaning is the existence of legal or legislative stipulations to protect the independence of the central bank from government interference. Nevertheless, the legal or formal independence has not reined in inflation under many circumstances (for instance, in the United States), while the central banks (for instance, in Japan, the Republic of South Korea and Singapore) almost without the legal independence all make the price very stable. As a matter of fact, the study indicates that in developing countries, there is no close relationship between the legal independence of a central bank and the average inflation rate or the changing rate of inflation. Another meaning of the independence of a central bank is related to the extent to which the fiscal sector interferes in the financial system. Fiscal interference means the requirement of making up the fiscal deficit by the central bank and the degree can be measured by the ratio of the financing of the central bank to the total fiscal deficit. In a number of countries, and in many developing countries in particular, the independence of the central bank in this sense is correlated with the low level of inflation. In countries whose central banks have relatively low legal independence such as Japan and Singapore, the low fiscal interference is the main cause of the low inflation. Furthermore, in explaining the aftermath of inflation, the development of financial markets appears more important than the legal independence of central banks in developing countries.

(4) Merits and demerits of direct and indirect control

The prerequisite of the independence of monetary policy is that the central bank has the discretion to employ and manipulate the instruments of monetary control in due course. The difference in the independence of the central bank in various countries tends to be reflected in the number of monetary control instruments available and their features. The difficulties encountered by developing countries in employing the vehicles of indirect control are often caused by the lack of full-fledged capital market and the instruments of the money market. A very good instance is the conditions in China. However, the more dependence is placed on the direct administrative monetary control and operation, the more limited will be the central bank's scope of activities.

The choice or design of monetary instruments must dovetail with the entire framework of monetary control, the reasons are: first, the chosen instruments of monetary control should be able to fulfil the pre-selected financial objective; secondly, different controlling programmes may affect the total amount of currency and the information accumulation in different manners. Therefore, the choice of the aggregate of objective should not be divorced from the controlling programme. Thirdly, the choice and employment of objective and programme will produce an influence upon the development of financial departments and further affect the operation of the entire economy. Historically, the major instrument of credit policy is to exert direct control on the credit business of the banking system. Obviously this is because the use of this controlling manner involves a simple method and produces clear effects. Given the relative weak status of the central bank, the implementation of the policies is likely to be more effective with the support of direct control from the government.

(5) Direct control often conflicts with financial development

Experts pointed out that the main dependence on direct control will bring about many drawbacks. To oblige banks to adopt the composition of assets they are reluctant to take so as to meet the upper limit of credit, and the requirements of reserve and current assets will make banks avoid (either evade or violate) direct control by all possible means. The chosen objective, as the value of the indicator of monetary policy, will also be impaired. Therefore, the major problem rests not with that the aggregate of objective is beyond control but with that the relations between this aggregate and the objective of policy are likely to be unstable or unpredictable.

If the control on credit quota actually obliges banks to keep excessive current assets, it will curb the intake of deposits and reduce the desire to save, thus weakening the effectiveness of monetary control. It is perhaps unlikely to promote deposits if only real deposit interest rates are set. This is because the institutions under control either do not welcome depositors or rack their brains to collect high handling fees or set up obstacles to deposit withdrawal, thereby increasing the "cost of dealings" and lowering the real rates they disburse. The simultaneous control of cost and quantity without side-effect is often not realized in actual implementation, despite people's constant efforts to use it as the objective of direct control.

First, it is difficult for the interest rate to play its role in the distribution of credit fund in this case. To distribute credit upper limit for each bank will even call for a political decision. Under the current structure in China, the feature of bargaining will exist for ever if the resources are allocated by government agencies. Thus, the overall credit control is often used for selective credit to subsidize or boost certain special sectors or regions. As this usually entails support from the central bank in the form of large amount of financing, the policy decision of the commercial banks becomes subordinate to the credit policy of the central bank. The arbitrarily political standard regarding credit policy often exerts more pressure on the relatively efficient banks and supports the inefficient institutions, thus affecting the quality of assets of the entire banking system.

Secondly, the lack of competition may hamper the forming of various interest rates which function effectively, and the development of financial instruments, and may also curb savings. On the other hand, the upper limit of credit may induce those financial intermediaries and financial instruments beyond control in a rush to compete with the institutions under control or even undermine their operations, thereby ultimately weakening monetary control through impairing the efficiency of credit control. Under such circumstances, the monetary authorities may be obliged to impose more stern credit control on the institutions under their control and enter a vicious cycle. This situation is especially severe in China. The financial institutions standing above the law and beyond control (or perhaps cannot be controlled) provide state-owned enterprises under soft budgetary restraints with loans, which weakens the government's ability to control monetary aggregate. Since the institutions beyond control are rarely subject to supervision and audit, the problem of liquidity arises very easily. They might easily disturb the financial system if they continue to go unmonitored.

Thirdly, the dependence on direct control is not beneficial to the development of money and capital markets which can raise the efficiency of resources allocation. If the markets develop in parallel with the approaches of direct control, they will provide other sources and channels of funds and thus weaken direct control. Without a formal securities market, commercial banks will inevitably become the major providers of short-term and revolving loans to public departments, while long-term financing needs the subsidies and refinancing from the government along with the supplementary loans from the financial institutions of development.

The requirements of reserve and current assets bear certain

administrative features, that is, they drive banks to go against the latter's own will to adopt some certain composition of assets. In spite of this, the requirements of reserve and current assets correspond with the objective of indirect control, that is, to control the financial aggregate by virtue of the supply of reserve money and market activities of economic organizations. Deposit reserve is useful, so to speak, at the beginning of the transition from the direct control means to the indirect means, but the frequency of its use should be gradually reduced as this requirement will curb the growth of financial market and the freeing of interest rates.

In a fairly free and more market-oriented structure, the money control framework based on indirect control includes three basic parts: The first part includes the ultimate objectives of monetary policy such as real GDP, price stability, balance of international payments and full employment. The second part includes the intermediate targets (variables) such as the aggregate of currency or credit. Observed from experience, they have kept stable and predictable relations within the ultimate objective of monetary policy. The third part concerns the operational variables such as interest rates of the money market or its liquidity level. They are under the direct control of the monetary authorities and have close relations with the variables of intermediate targets of monetary policy.

In this framework, the monetary authorities manage operational variables, while the market mechanism decides the structure of deposit interest rates and the distribution of credit. The central bank brings the interest rates of the money market under control by managing the savings money, which is the main instrument of monetary control. In this system, control is not materialized by the requirements of compulsory reserve and current assets. The central bank adjusts the deficiencies of reserve or the excess liquidity in the banking system only by managing its own assets and liabilities and controlling the conditions of its willingness to provide or take in funds. In other words, the operation of indirect instruments of monetary policy, such as the auction of treasury bonds and rediscount by the central bank will change the amount of cash reserve of the banking system by affecting the supply and demand of reserve money. Other objectives were also used but their effects were not ideal. To make the interest rate the objective of control will affect the efficacy of a monetary policy because the nominal interest can hardly reflect the real one, especially in an environment of prolonged and erratic inflationary expectations.

The objective of exchange rate may be very important in an open economy or an economy dependent upon foreign trade. This is mainly because the capital flow caused by abnormal fluctuations of the exchange rate will lead to the instability of exchange rate and the economy. What must be pointed out is that if monetary control depends upon the reserve management of the bank, there are two possible measures of policy whose results are very opposite; the central bank will decide the types of changes to be faced and take the proper policy measure. If the changes of bank reserve originate from the factors relating to economic growth, then, the central bank may maintain a relatively inelastic reserve supply and realize more effectively its ultimate objectives, that is, the real economy and inflation. However, if the changes mainly come from the demand for money, the maintenance of a relatively flexible reserve supply will be conducive to realizing the ultimate objectives.

In the use of indirect control, we may use two methods to analyze the framework of monetary control. One is the method of intermediate targets. By using intermediate targets (such as the definitions of various kinds of money supply), the central bank decides the instruments of monetary policy and influences the expectations and activities of economic organizations. Historically, the intermediate targets should be good indicators of the ultimate policy objectives. The other is a financial planning method based on the following accounting equation (essentially the formula of relationship of the balance sheet): The change of money stock (M) equals the sum of its domestic and foreign changes. The foreign portion means the net foreign assets (NFA) expressed by currency, and the domestic portion means net domestic assets (NDA); $dM=dNFA+dNDA$. This equation is used to explain different definitions of money. That defined in the balance sheets of the central bank and the banking system are the most commonly used two.

Assuming that money is decided by demand and is the function of several key variables such as yield (y), interest rate (r) and price (p), then the net foreign assets (NFA) may be expressed as the difference between the change in the money stock (by definition it equals the change in the nominal demand of currency) and that in the net domestic assets (NDA): $dNFA = dM - dNDA = dMd = f(y,r,p)$. In this analysis if the central bank alone controls the net domestic assets (NDA), it can manage the net foreign assets (NFA). The net domestic assets can be broken down into the net claims on public departments in connection with the fiscal account and the net claims on private departments.

The main difference between the two methods of analysis is: The method of intermediate targets is very useful as the index of the pressure of the overall resources, while the financial planning method is usually concerned with the distribution of resources between the domestic and external sources. In the event of a stable money demand, the pressure of resources may be managed through the planning of the domestic and external sources.

The main content of the operational framework of indirect monetary control is the management of reserve money. The supply and demand of reserve money can be managed by a flexible operational method so that it can coordinate with the balance of the preventive reserve at the interest rate of the money market. The main instruments which can be flexibly used include the auction of treasury bonds, rediscount policy and deposit reserve. The choice of using money control rests on the sensitivity of the banks and customers to interest rates and on the extent to which the money and capital markets grow.

A series of arrangements about structure and a series of policy measures must be made if indirect instruments are employed in the framework of monetary control. In other words, if monetary reform involves the shift to indirect control, this calls for the whole set of reform in the structure and policy.

First, money and capital markets shall be fostered in which the central bank may and must play a key role. The premise of this suggestion includes the enactment of a whole set of basic laws with detailed stipulations on bonds, securities and notes, detailed explanations of their features and the conditions of their transfer and circulation. It is necessary to build up various mechanisms enabling people to obtain enough information to judge the risks of various financial instruments; it is also necessary to take steps to carry out standardized management to reduce the above risks. It is necessary to set up a securities dealers' network, exercise intensified management and, in the meantime, to establish a mechanism whereby provisional financing can be provided for securities dealers such as the securities repurchase agreement at market interest rates. The central bank may play a vital role in all these aspects.

After the burgeoning development of money and capital markets, the central bank must proceed from the management of government bonds to boost the further development of these markets. This is because the procedure and technique of government borrowing and the fixing of interest rates for internal debts all exert an enormous influence on the entire level of interest rates and the efficiency of financial sectors. The precondition for private financing institutions and the market to maintain competitiveness and efficiency is the effective structural frame of managing government debts.

Second, to reinforce the building up of a market structure. If there is only feeble and incomplete competition among financial institutions, monopoly profit will be produced and the development of new instruments and new markets will be hampered. Specific policies must be framed to stimulate competitions, including the removal of various barriers preventing the new financial institutions from entering the market and the repeal of administrative and regulatory rules of dividing the scope of businesses and markets for various financial institutions. With the decontrol of interest rates and the gradual change of distributing credit through the market, tremendously different influences will be produced on the reliability of certain enterprises and borrowers, especially under conditions of loose credit discipline and serious default of loans (as in China). Therefore, it is perhaps necessary to implement a plan of adjustment and reorganization. Audit and supervision need to be enormously strengthened to ensure the soundness, reputation and justice of the financial system. The above brand-new or reformed systems of legislation and° supervision must be both mobile and flexible to suit the development of money and capital markets and broad enough to cover new types of financial activities.

Bank supervision is generally invested in the central bank in most developing countries. In most developed countries, an independent organ often shoulders the task, though it is less rare that the central bank and other organs share this responsibility. It tends to be the best choice to build up an independent control organ so as to assume effective supervision.

2. The Central Bank and Monetary Policy

1) The Experience of History Has Fully Proved That There Is Very Strong Correlation Between the Independence of the Central Bank and Inflation Control

Since China's economy is still in the transitional stage, the reliability of monetary policy is still not urgent, but it should not go unnoticed. With the steady progress of market-oriented reform, with the continued brisk development of non-state-owned sectors, with the daily economic opening to the outside world, the ever closer economic links with other nations and with the growth of the non-state-owned financial intermediaries based upon market, the reliability of monetary policy will inevitably become more and more important in the future.

What statesmen and government leaders hanker after tends to go against sustained anti-inflationary policies. Therefore, the discipline of monetary policy can be best ensured only by the arrangements in a system of leaving the formulating and implementation of a monetary policy to independent authorities separate from the government. Now, people almost generally believe that an independent central bank is the precondition of a disciplined monetary policy; therefore, it is also the precondition of inflation control and price stability on the premise of not sacrificing the policy makers' ability to make responses to and their power to deal with the unexpected happenings. From this angle, the voice for strengthening the independence of the central bank is at a highest pitch in China, for, as stated above, the pressure and the range of interference from different groups of interests (various departments and local governments) are sizable.

The lack of independence of the central bank has become the main structural and restrictive element impeding the effective enactment and implementation of the monetary policy. China's monetary policy is highly subordinate to and subject to the fiscal policy and the economic developmental goal of the government. And more important, the lack of independence of monetary policy of the central bank is of distinct Chinese characteristic. Evidently, the central bank has no power to decide the monetary policy. Moreover, (after the approval by the State Council) even the implementation and operation of the monetary policy are clearly interfered by local sectors. The officials of the local branches tend to be at the command of local government rather than head office. Therefore, China's central bank is in a difficult position: on one hand, the central government puts forward various requirements, on the other, the local branches do not toe the line. The core of the question is that the ministries, commissions and local governments know that as the central bank is not independent and is subordinate to other departments of the government, their pressure for loans can work and indeed it does work. An independent central bank is important to break the communicating mechanism of loan pressure.

As far as the case in China is concerned, another benefit of the independence of the central bank is that independent monetary authorities can exercise monitoring and balancing functions with regard to other sectors of the government. China's macroeconomic instability in the latter part of the 1980s should be blamed to a great extent on the policy of high growth. It is just because the People's Bank was almost absolutely obedient to the government that this policy of high growth could materialize. If the People's Bank had enjoyed stronger independence at that time, the ability of government to depart from its announced policy of steady growth would have been better restricted. Especially, if there had been legal provisions restricting the central bank's power to make up the government's financial deficit, the arbitrary policy measures of government would have been controlled.

The Chinese government is concerned with how to make the state manage its economy effectively and purposefully so as to achieve harmonious growth. Therefore it needs a clarified and clear definition of an independent central bank and of "its relationship with the government."

Although the basic theoretical basis and meaning of the notion of "independence of the central bank" is perhaps clear, this term still may be a little misleading. A demarcation line can be drawn between the independence of the central bank in making monetary policy decisions and that of monetary policy. Some people proposed the use of more exact notion, that is, "the independence (of the central bank) within the government," rather than "independent from the government." According to the former meaning, the central bank provides independent professional consulting, and meanwhile has the right to make public and explain its policy differences with other departments of the government. The central bank remains a part of the government, and the ultimate responsibilities of economic policies and economic operation (including those of the monetary sector) are borne by the governments or parliament. Therefore, some people proposed adopting "autonomy" or "prudent autonomy" of the central bank or monetary policy in place of "independence" which falls short of the connotation of restraint or responsibility.

Even if the independence of a central bank can be more correctly construed as autonomy within a government, an independent or autonomous central bank may also raise a series of questions calling for attention and discussion. The most important one is the potential and quite possible conflict between monetary policy and certain parts of the government's extensive economic plan. Obviously, the monetary policy must be subject to the government's overall policy or development strategy. The effectiveness of monetary policy is determined by other fields and by the reliability of the overall government policy. In addition, if people hold that the monetary policy and other government policies are inconsistent with one another and irreconcilable, then the reliability of monetary policy may also be jeopardised. If the independent central bank follows a tight monetary policy, and the government's economic plan has brought about huge fiscal deficits in consecutive years, either the monetary policy or the fiscal one must make a concession to the other. Whichever makes the concession will produce very different effects on inflation. The mutual inconsistency of policies will itself lead to uncertainty.

Besides, like other bureaucratic organs, an independent central bank is also easily subject to pressure and influence of vested interests (as the case of U.S. Federal Reserve Bank) or needs to avoid conflicts with the government (as the case of Bundesbank). Therefore, the independence of central bank may also possibly lead to the decreased reliability of monetary policy and to inflation. This is the same with the lack of independence on the part of the central bank. In this respect, several reasons can be put forth and quite a lot of examples can be given. The existence of the above dangers, however, does not sufficiently constitute the argument against the central bank's independence. On the contrary, these dangers have revealed that it is necessary to build up various mechanisms and procedures to ensure consistency and coordination between the central bank and the government, and to end effectively the conflicts between the monetary policy and other (the fiscal in particular) policies.

2) Possible Steps Effecting the Relative Independence of China's Central Bank

The relative independence of the central bank, as an instrument for promoting the discipline of monetary policy in China, can be conveniently included in the existent train of thought in China's reform. We want to make especial mention of the principle of operational autonomy guiding the reform of China's state-owned enterprises. The application of this notion to the independence of the central bank, if a stronger explanation is made, means that the People's Bank of China will have the right both to make and carry out monetary policy. If a rather weak explanation is given, it means that the bank enjoys only the autonomy of carrying out or implementing monetary policy, or the autonomy of implementing monetary policy is given to the bank. Even if it means the latter, the rather weak power, this will be much better than the present situation and certainly promote the consistency of monetary policy.

The central bank's operational autonomy in implementing its monetary policy may be safeguarded by government legislation. The above legislation represents "contracting" between the government and the central bank. Contracting can designate the targets of money supply and credit aggregate and the principle of price stability. If initially full confidence is lacking, the granting autonomy to the central bank may be set for a brief period of time, say one year. But the period of time in which the People's Bank is authorized to carry out monetary policy on its own will be long enough to let the policy yield results. After a period of time, confidence will grow gradually and the contracting period may be extended accordingly. Contracting aims mainly at ensuring the independence of the monetary authorities in implementing the policy, thus separating it (along with the government) from the arbitrary interference. During the contracting period, the government cannot change the contracting terms without the parliamentary approval.

The important fact worth emphasizing is that the independence of central bank should be an actual independence. We often observe that in many cases there is divergences between the stipulations in law and in theory, and the real practice. Many study results indicate: First, the actual independence of the central bank is determined by many features of the system. Second, informal factors (such as the personality of the governor of the central bank, and the informal contacts among its governor, directors and the administrative officials) will greatly affect the extent of the actual independence of the central bank. Study reports reveal that even if the independence of the central bank in theory has been ensured, the legal system in practice may still not cover the strong influence and interference exerted by the political leaders. Moreover, the reliability and results of the monetary policy are often greatly decided by invisible factors, such as the personality of the governor of the central bank or the head of government. In Britain, the Bank of England is the central bank with the least independence in the developed countries (in practice or in law), however, since there exists a tradition of non-frequent or excessive interference by the government, it actually enjoys great independence.

Nevertheless, these informal factors are too delicate to become the foundation stone for ensuring the liability of monetary policy. To maintain the nominal independence of the central bank calls for several indispensable formal and informal arrangements. To ensure real independence, however, the details of the arrangements play a decisive role.

The formal responsibility of monetary policy and the resolution of conflicts. The central bank must constantly consult with the government in implementing the monetary policy in order to ensure mutual unanimity between the monetary policy and other aspects of government economic policies. As to the concrete arrangements of consultations, the practices differ greatly. A strongly independent central bank, which still has consultation with the government included into its formal duties, should support the government's economic policy only if the policy corresponds with the bank's open objective of maintaining price stability. A less independent central bank is an implementing agency and a key brain tank of government monetary policy. With regard to a central bank between the above two kinds, it is independent from the administrative departments in theory, but has the responsibility to make regular report of its work to parliament.

The stronger the independence of the central bank, the more it is necessary to set up a mechanism for solving policy conflicts. This is not only for promoting the consistency of policy but also for minimizing the risk of using informal means to limit the legal independence of the central bank by the government. The arrangements for solving conflicts endow the central bank with considerable policy autonomy, but the central bank will also obey the open interference of the government in certain forms so as to make their respective responsibilities transparent in case of a policy discrepancy and an ultimate decision. Only if there is the mechanism for the solution to conflicts, the government tends not to exercise the power to give orders even if it has it. This is because the mechanism effectively restricts the government during the frequent consultations between the government and the central bank. Moreover, the mechanism also effectively encourages both sides to resolve their disputes before publicly issuing a direct order and embarking on the procedures of solving conflicts.

Legal objective. The extent of the independence of the central bank tends to link up with the breadth of the legal objective. The narrower the definition of the legal macro-economic objective (usually it focuses on the stability of prices and exchange rate), the bigger the extent of the independence of central bank. When the central bank has less independence, the scope of legal objective tends to be quite wide. The broad range of objectives or multiple objectives assigned to the central bank tend to jeopardize the reliability of its monetary policy. The reasons are: First, the case allows the authorities to change its policies within a very wide range of objectives (likely to be mutual inconsistent internally), or change its emphasis, thus further reducing the transparency of monetary policy. Second, it is hard for one instrument of monetary policy to achieve several objectives (often in contradiction with one other) at the same time. Third, it is more and more doubtful as to whether the operation of monetary policy can realize the steady growth of real sectorial aggregate. Consequently the task of the monetary policy shall be limited only to the creation of an environment ensuring price stability so as to guarantee the fulfilment of the objectives of output and employment. Fourth, only if the monetary policy includes multiple macro-economic objectives, does the central bank become like any other governmental sectors in actually carrying out the same set of objectives with different permutations and combinations.

In this case, the central bank or the monetary policy has no reason at all to demand independence.

To define the legal objective narrowly (for instance, price stability) or to differentiate the central bank clearly from administrative government departments means the extensive independence of the central bank. The legal restrictions of the budgetary financing of the central bank (either direct overdraft or the purchase of treasury bonds from the primary market) determine the extent of actual independence enjoyed by the central bank and the monetary policy. If restrictions on the central bank's financing for the government apply to all direct overdrafts of the Ministry of Finance, are computed at the percentage of the government's revenue rather than its expenditure, and permit no breach or change without the approval of the parliament, the restrictions will reach the most stringent extent.

Interpretation and supervision of the policy. It is necessary to build up the mechanism to interpret and supervise monetary policy. This is not only to give a guarantee to the public and maintain transparency, but also to encourage the central bank to keep the motivating force to fulfil the announced objective. Perhaps China may draw on the method of New Zealand. Instead of generally placing the responsibility on the Reserve Bank of New Zealand (the central bank), the legislative authorities of New Zealand focuses its attention on the president of the bank. The mechanism requires that the president realize the objective of the policy he announced during his tenure of office and put this content in his "contract of achievements" with the prime minister. The Reserve Bank of New Zealand submits semi-annual and annual statements of policy to the prime minister (to be put forward before parliament) for due supervision. Subsequently, an outside organ makes extensive "auditing of achievements," and the prime minister has the power to summon this organ.

Those central banks with less independence tend to fall short of the strong interpreting mechanism. In this instance, interpretation and supervision are generally completed through the superintendence of the parliament. The head and senior officials of the central bank will be called to respond to the questions posed by members of parliament. Interpretation and supervision may also be completed through the fulfilment and publication of the targets of monetary aggregate (sometimes other targets).

The role, composition, appointment and removal of the board of directors (its members) of the central bank. The role and composition of the board of the central bank may determine the nature of the relationship between the central bank and the government. This is especially so when the board serves as the formal channel of the government for affecting the policy decision of the central bank.

In most countries, the government may actually appoint most, if not all, members of the board of directors of the central bank and its committee. Sometimes, it may appoint non-official members to represent the government. The board members on behalf of the government may request the board to postpone its decisions, or reconsider them. However, some countries have given up the practice of directly sending government representatives to the board. In most countries, a major standard guiding the formation of the board is to enlarge the representation of regions and sectors.

The central bank with greater independence tends to impose more restrictions on the government's power of appointment and replacement. The restrictions take the following forms: A proportion is fixed for board members not appointed by the government, the candidates are not recommended or nominated by the government, the tenure does not coincide with the electoral cycle and the tenures of the board members are staggered. This aims at preventing the government from controlling the board through its appointed members. Even in a less independent central bank, restrictions are also effective. The results of study indicate that the length of tenure of the member on the board of the central bank varies inversely with the inflation rate.

In many countries, the dismissal of the president of the central bank tends to be attributed to technical reasons (for instance, bankruptcy, crime and conflict of interests) but not to other clearly observed causes (such as political reasons). In Japan, the cabinet may replace the president or vice presidents of the central bank for political reasons but not members of the board.

Restrictions on government financing. To restrict legally the central bank from financing the government is an important intrinsic element of ensuring the independence of the central bank and monetary policy. The restrictions may adopt the following forms: to prohibit the provision of direct or indirect financing for the public expenditures through overdraft or the purchase of bonds issued by the government or its agencies; to strictly restrain the central bank from giving overdrafts to the government, but allow the central bank to purchase government bonds in the normal course of open market operations. An agreement is reached between the central bank and the government beforehand on the terms of restrictions, but subject to approval by the parliament (sometimes retroactively).

However, there are considerable drawbacks in legally restricting the central bank from financing the government. Firstly, the above restrictions can be circumvented by different means. Secondly, since the central bank perhaps needs to obtain government bonds for its business of currency management, so it is neither wise nor feasible to limit legally the central bank from issuing any loans to the government. Thirdly, the government can instruct the central bank to inject funds through other channels (such as to purchase the bonds of the private sector), thereby enabling the government to borrow money from the private sector. Case studies indicate that legal restrictions do not produce good results when the central bank has no independence, whereas restrictions are unnecessary when it is independent. The major merit of restrictions is that it can help restrain the monetary field when the central bank has little or no independence and the financial market is relatively less developed.

The budgetary independence of the central bank. Apart from the independence of monetary policy, central banks in developed countries enjoy broad financial independence. They have the ability to determine their own outlays and make up their deficits by issuing their obligations. The budgetary independence of the central bank involves the following questions: First, to support the independence of policy, what is the necessary extent of financial independence? Second, what is the form of the funds? The financial stimulus mechanism of the central bank shall be consistent with the objective of monetary stability. Third, with regard to the central bank enjoying budgetary independence, how does it ensure its financial efficiency?

3. The Shift of Monetary Policy to Market Economy

How does China's monetary policy suit the requirements of market economy? Experts made some constructive proposals:

1) Scientific Formulating of Intermediate Targets of Monetary Policy

Money supply is generally chosen as one of the intermediate targets of monetary policy in Western countries. Influenced by its traditional structure, China has long made credit plan and credit scale the main intermediate targets of monetary policy, which calls for a set of fairly scientific methods in fixing and quantifying the scale. It is unrealistic to abandon entirely the control of credit scale at the present stage when the instruments of financial indirect control are imperfect. Moreover, ours is a developing country with insufficient funds and resources, and without control over the credit scale, bank credit would easily get out of control and lead to inflation. However, control of the planned credit scale has been bereft of effectiveness to some extent and there is a far cry between the amount of annual planned scale and the results of its implementation. In effect our money supply is open-ended.

To fix the credit scale scientifically, the formulating procedure of an annual credit plan should change from "start from grass roots" to "start from the top level," fixing the "rational scale" of credit expansion from the very beginning. In fixing the new scale of increased loans, detailed and specific investigation and analyses shall be made in the light of the law of money circulation, and comprehensive consideration be given to the changes of economic factors such as the changes in commodity growth rate, the speed of money circulation, population, the shares held by various forms of ownership and geographical distribution of economic areas. The scale should be fixed on the basis of quantitative analysis by using computing instruments and scientific methods, replacing the present method of purely following the targets. Moreover, base money and short-term interest rates may be chosen as the monitor indicators of the intermediate targets of monetary policy, and in the process of implementing the monetary policy, the changes of the two indicators shall be emphasized intentionally to make the intermediate targets of China's monetary policy shift to the two indicators.

2) Choice of Instruments of Monetary Policy: Combined Use of Direct and Indirect Means of Control.

In addition to the use of general instruments of monetary policy like deposit reserve, rediscount and open-market operations, the scale of newly-added loans should be chosen as the means of direct credit control; the form of credit distribution should be adopted to restrict the credit creation of commercial banks such as the rationing of reissued loans and the restriction on the proportion of rediscount. A supporting measure of reform is to substitute the clearing centre of the central bank for the inter-branch system of a specialized bank, which enables the central bank to muster the changes of the accounts of financial institutions as reference for rationing reissued loans. Control of the credit plan and management of the cash plan should be abandoned, and overall assets and liabilities management, risk management, and current assets ratio management of commercial banks and non-bank financial institutions should be carried out. The adjustment of money supply is mainly carried out by changes in the ratio of deposit reserve, interest rate, and the securities business on the financial market. This reform measures may reach the following results:

First, it may bring unlimited expansion of the credit scale under control but not of a rigid control, forming an elastic control invigorating a micro economy. Second, it may enlarge the proportion of indirect control, promoting the building up and perfection of various means of indirect control. Third, the system of administrative rationing of re-lending may play a guiding role in fund allocation by the central bank's direct participation, which is beneficial to implementing the state industrial policy and adjusting the economic structure.

3) Improving the System of Deposit Reserve

The main role of the legal deposit reserve aims at restricting credit expansion and money increase. From the very beginning, China's deposit reserve system has the function of adjusting both fund structure and payment reserve through the central bank. The legal rate of deposit reserve is too high without classification (flatly 13 percent), and one fraction of the reserve is used in issuing various special loans which are mostly policy-oriented ones with lower results, long terms and big risks. The partial use of deposit reserve itself carries the hidden danger of credit expansion and inflation. Besides, the central bank often issue loans to specialized banks with deposit reserve at a premium much higher than the legal one, this encourages the specialized banks to expand credit at a still larger rate, which causes the growth of the money supply far in excess of the GNP (the annual average growth of GNP was 10 percent whereas that of money supply 20 percent since 1979) and deprives the reserve of its original meaning. Therefore, the perfection of the reserve system means: First, the central bank should not use deposit reserve to grant special loans and adjust fund structure. Second, to build up multi-tier reserve rates and adjust them in due course, thus making them real forceful instruments of the indirect financial macro-control.

4) Creating Vigorous Conditions to Develop Discount and Rediscount Business

The main function of the rediscount policy of the central banks in Western countries rests on the rediscount rate's role to guide the level of market interest rates, and exemplary or market signalling role of the policy. Given the lack of standardized form of commercial credit (mostly credit of account record and oral credit), occasional use of notes in socioeconomic transactions, and the absence of marketized interest rate, it is still difficult for China's central bank to employ this instrument of monetary policy.

The under-development of China's discount market is restricted to a great extent by the financial system such as the non-enterprise operation of specialized banks, the planned control of credit scale and the vertical distribution of specialized banks funds; the specialized banks have neither internal motivating force nor external pressure to conduct the discount business. With the progress of the bank's reform to practise enterprise operation and improve macro-financial regulation, the above hampering factors will be gradually removed. The tapping and development of traditional business will inevitably be realized when conditions are ripe. At present, what should be done is to emphasize the management of standardized commercial credit, increase its use of notes, strengthen the liquidity of commercial notes and set up and create the basis and conditions of rediscount business.

5) Starting Open Market Operations at an Opportune Time

The start of open market operation helps the central bank establish its initiative status in receiving and paying out base currency, and eliminates the "back-extorting" mechanism whereby banks and other financial institutions seek loans from the central bank. Below are three approaches available in the open-market operation of the central bank:

First, use treasury debts as financing instruments, allowing domestic leading banks and financial institutions to hold newly issued treasury debt certificates, and transforming the accumulated bank balances of overdraft and borrowing owed by the treasury into medium- and long-term treasury bonds, which the central bank may purchase and sell out in the time of the austerity or relaxation of money supply. Meanwhile, transform the loans owed by the treasury to the central bank into securities providing convenient instruments for the government to repay the loans in better fiscal years (for instance, the government may buy back these bonds in installments to reduce its deficits). Second, issue long-term financing certificates of the central bank.

The financing certificates can enter the money market for transfer, banks and other financial institutions are asked first to buy the certificates pro rata, and the certificates are not allowed to be held by individuals or used as currency for circulation. Subsequently, the central bank can regularly issue financing certificates at different interest rates and periods and buy back them on the secondary market at any time. The interest rate and market price of the financing certificate shall shape the benchmark of interest rate policy. Third, the central bank may enter the domestic market of foreign exchange to conduct exchange business thereby serving the policy of exchange rate and regulating the money supply. The approach may serve as a supplement to the two above.

6) Rational Coordination Between Monetary Policy and Fiscal Policy

According to some experts, monetary policy and fiscal policy are two major instruments of policy with which the government can realize its macro-economic control under the conditions of market economy. Rational policy coordination requires: Monetary policy control the equilibrium of social total demand and total supply and maintain the currency stable so as to let the economy operate in a stable price system. The fiscal policy shall ensure the social fairness and interfere properly in the major economic structure for the long-run interests of the social public.

The market is the foundation of allocating social resources in the market economy. When inflation exists, neither does the price reflect exactly the scarcity of resources nor can investors correctly judge future profits, so optimizing the allocation of resources is out of the question. To let the monetary policy bear the function of readjusting the economic structure calls for the input of huge funds, which may often bring about excessive money supply, lead to inflation and affect economic stability.

Within financial macro-control in China, the biggest problem is that the central bank directly bears policy-oriented loans for economic structural readjustment. Through the indirect form of issuing loans by specialized banks, the central bank directly uses base currency to invest in key economic sectors or projects, which badly need funds. As a result, the central bank faces the rigid mechanism of paying out its base currency without repayment and cannot use the increase and decrease of base currency to control flexibly money supply. Consequently, in the assets structure of the People's Bank of China, direct credit loans to financial institutions (mainly state-owned specialized banks) account for the largest percentage as shown in the following table:

Table of Assets Structure of the People's Bank of China (according to balances)

	Loans to financial institutions	Overdraft and loans by fiscal sectors	Assets of gold and foreign exchange	Direct loans
1985	77.9	13.6	2.0	2.5
1986	78.2	14.0	1.2	3.5
1987	73.2	16.6	1.1	4.4
1988	74.9	15.3	1.7	6.7
1989	72.9	13.7	4.5	5.6
1990	70.0	12.5	8.2	5.4
1991	66.6	13.1	13.6	4.9
1992	67.8	12.2	11.0	5.6

Source: 1992 Annual Report of the People's Bank of China

A major reason for employing administrative management of credit scale in China is because monetary policy bears the task of adjusting economic structure. Under the conditions of market economy, the lending amount of commercial banks shall be decided by their absorbed deposits, as the usual saying "more deposits, more credits." Nevertheless, there are more deposits in the economically developed coastal provinces in China and less deposits in the central and western regions that urgently need the input of funds. According to the "more deposits, more credits" principle, more credit funds will go to the coastal areas, thereby deepening the contradiction of uneven economic development in various places. To avoid this situation, the People's Bank of China shoulders the heavy task of adjusting regional economic imbalance.

The 13 percent of legal reserve of Chinese financial institutions is used for adjusting the regional imbalance of funds and not as reserve for payments, while the normal deposits in the People's Bank put by financial institutions are used as reserve for payments. As to the gap between coastal areas and interior regions, 13 percent of reserve is far from enough to bridge this gap. The People's Bank adopts as remedy the method of limiting the credit scale. The strong demand by coastal provinces for fund management on regional basis reflects the contradiction of more deposits but less credits. The People's Bank cannot abolish the credit scale and allow the coastal areas to extend more credit based on their more deposits because of the contradiction that the hinterland and western areas want to obtain more credit with less deposits. The heavy task of adjusting regional economic structure places the People's Bank in a dilemma.

To let the monetary policy bear the heavy task of adjusting the economic structure makes it difficult to control base currency, and hinders the realization of the principle of more deposits, more credits. Finally the central bank has to control credit scale mainly by administrative methods, and thus restricts the most important factor in market economy, funds flow according to the market law. The result must be the reduced efficiency of resources allocation.

Public finance represents the state's interests; to ensure the normal operation of the state and social stability, it should manage money matters and uphold social justice for the state. Socioeconomic structure involves the long-term development of society; however, the investments in certain matters beneficial to social long-term interests or to the interests of social public cannot achieve the social average rate of return. This kind of investment can only be borne by the fiscal sectors on behalf of social interests. The large-scale fund input supported by the state can rapidly change the economic structure of a country, and with the perfection of market and the entry of economy into benign cycle, the percentage of government input to funds can be gradually reduced. The Japanese government of post World War II successfully employed its investment and financing system in support of the high-speed growth of Japanese economy and its adjustment of structure.

The investment and financing funds of the government can be raised by means of taxation and state credit.

7) Building Up the Structure of Investment and Financing of the Government to Bear the Macro-control of Economic Structure

Some experts hold that the functions of China's monetary and fiscal policies should be definite, and the fiscal investment and financing institutions should be included in the financial system. Experts propose that to achieve macro-control of economic structure, China may draw on the experience of Japan in setting up its fiscal system of investment and financing. The funds of this system may be classified in two categories by their uses: One is state capital input which may be listed as state-owned assets and managed by operating intermediaries of assets, the other is funds to be used with compensation and employed through policy-oriented financial institutions. The funds of the fiscal investment and financing system may come from the following sources: (a) outlays of economic construction from fiscal sectors; (b) the centralized funds with compensation by fiscal sectors, such as surpluses of postal savings and social insurance funds; (c) treasury bonds and government guaranteed bonds.

The establishment and operation of policy-oriented financial institutions shall adhere to the following principles:

(1) The scope of using policy-oriented finance should be narrowed with energetic efforts. In China this scope is so wide that policy-oriented loans include those which have been granted by many financial institutions according to guidance of the government's industrial policies and that of the credit policy of the People's Bank. In a strict sense, policy-oriented loans, refer-

ring only to the loans to the projects which need long-term investment, cannot bear the normal market interest rate but bring huge benefits to society. In step with the reform of foreign trade structure, the reform of the purchase and marketing structure of farm and sideline products and the readjustment of price relations, the future policy-oriented loans are mainly used for the construction of infrastructural facilities and base industries, including rural infrastructural facilities, and the stockpiling of important materials including farm produce.

(2) Adhere to repayment of principal and interest and perform the non-profit operation. The policy-oriented loan is not a government allocation and the project using this kind of loan must have the ability to repay principal and interest. If the project cannot repay even the principal, it needs an allocation. The interest rate of policy-oriented loans may be a little lower than the market rate, but policy-oriented financial institutions must be permitted to operate at the break-even point, keeping their rates at the central bank's benchmark rate. At the current price level in China, many infrastructural facilities and base trades have very low capacity to bear interest, and this can be solved through the fiscal interest subsidy in the transitional stage and ultimately through price reform.

(3) Policy-oriented financial institutions should make their own decision and assume their own risks under the guidance of industrial policy and planning of the government. The biggest problem in the operation of planned economy is that no one bears the ultimate economic responsibility for decision made on the project. To guide the flow of social funds by financial means aims at establishing a mechanism of unifying responsibility, power and interests.

(4) A policy-oriented financial institution should be a capable and simplified one, and place its emphasis on the choice of the direction of fund employment; its detailed business can be handled through market bidding and through commercial financial institutions. In view of the conditions in China, the policy-oriented financial institutions may be first set up in the fields of capital construction and agriculture.

8) To Accelerate the Transforming of Specialized State Banks to State-owned Commercial Banks, Develop the Capital Market, Set Up the Risk Restraint Mechanism for Financial Institutions and Form a Marketized Fine-tuning Mechanism of Economic Structure

It is the direction of reform to let funds flow to the high profit earning trades through banks and the capital market so as to realize the optimal allocation of social resources. It is also the main method of fully utilizing the market mechanism to boost economic development. To set up such a mechanism, it is necessary first to let the state-owned specialized banks separate their policy-oriented functions from commercial ones, allow them really to operate on the principles of profitability, security and liquidity, and enable them to make flexible and correct response to the market signal. Second, set up a self-restrained capital market. The main problem of the present abnormal development of the capital market in China originates from the fact that the risks of investment and enterprise operation are not really borne by the investors, but are shifted to the state by various means. Hence the trend of unlimited expansion on the capital market. Third, set up an elastic system to control bank credit. Under the condition of unchanged demand for social money supply, when the share of the social investment through capital market grows, bank credit shall be properly reduced. This provides the basis of effectively realizing optimized readjustment of economic structure. Under the situation of inflated credit, expansion in the old framework and old structure often reappears.

Chapter VI
Going to Convertible Currency

1. Background of Theory and Positivism

The convertibility of a currency refers to its ability to convert into other currencies or means of payment. In accordance with the extent of convertibility, currencies can be divided into three categories: freely convertible, limited convertible and inconvertible ones. The Articles of Agreement of the International Monetary Fund (IMF) provides that if a country imposes no restrictions on the transfer of funds in the international current account, uses no discriminative monetary policy or multiple exchange rates and has the duty to exchange the currency of another member country, at the latter's request anytime, back to its own currency accumulated on the latter's current account, its currency is freely convertible. A freely convertible currency does not necessarily become an internationally recognized hard currency, the hardiness of a currency is also determined by such elements as universality and acceptability in international use. But the first and foremost premise of a hard currency is its free convertibility.

Article VIII and Article XIV of the Articles of Agreement of the Fund is aimed at the convertibility of a currency. Section 2 of Article VIII provides that, without the permission of the Fund, its members allow no restrictions to be imposed on their payments and transfer of international trade under current account; Section 3 provides that its members do not allow the conducting of any discriminative monetary arrangements or multiple monetary business; Section 4 provides that the convertibility of the currencies in the hands of overseas holders should be maintained so as to keep them in balance. It is generally held that the currencies of its member states who agree to accept the duties as listed in Article VIII are convertible. Article XIV puts forward transitional measures and permits its members to exercise certain restrictions. Members complying with Article VIII and members with Article XIV differ in their duties on the foreign exchange markets. Freely convertible currencies can thereby be classified as fully convertible and limited ones.

Limited exchange of currency is an approach between the freely convertible and inconvertible. At present many countries have adopted this form, including free conversion of non-residents (residents abroad), regional free convertibility, free convertibility under the current account of balance of payments, and free exchange of capital transfer. Although China has exercised rather strict foreign exchange control, it also permits currency exchange within certain limits. In this sense, the convertibility of Renminbi is actually a first step in making Renminbi gradually become freely convertible.

1) Convertibility of Currency Calls for Rationalization of Exchange Rate

The convertibility of currency is part of an exchange rate policy. It is inseparably interconnected with the floating equilibrium rate of exchange. The equilibrium of an exchange rate and the resulting practice of floating management are the prerequisite of the convertibility of currency, while the elevating of the exchangeable degree of currency is conducive to the realization and persistence of the freely floating exchange rate.

The exchange rate is a price, an important price with a comprehensive significance and the general attribute of price. On the part of a commodity, the equilibrium price can realize market clearance, that is, achieving balance between supply and demand. If a price is lower than the equilibrium price, then rationing or queuing is bound to appear, and the transactions are not free or not fully free. If a price is higher than the equilibrium price, overstock will occur and administrative restrictions will have to be adopted to decrease output, cut back stockpiling or limit the entry in and competition of the market, that is, to restrict the freedom of economic entities. Like the law of commodity price, without the rationalization of an exchange rate, there will be no freedom of conversion. And because of the high importance of foreign exchange to the economy of a country, the government is bound to emphasize the balance of foreign exchange. If the exchange rate cannot guarantee the balance between the supply of and demand for foreign exchange, the government will inevitably resort to other means of management, which tends to restrict the freedom of economic activities.

The notion of equilibrium exchange rate should be adopted in the rationalization of exchange rate, which can promote and ensure the balance of international payments. This rate may be decided upon by the supply-and-demand law in the market or by the government which may fix the rate approximately at a point of equilibrium of supply and demand according to a market signal and administer floating management any time according to the change in the actual conditions. If the exchange rate is not one based on balance between demand and supply, certain amounts of money will seek a trade at another point of equilibrium of supply and demand, forming two kinds of exchange rates in the actual operation or a black market exchange rate, and thus the convertibility of the currency concerned will be in doubt. An equilibrium rate of exchange can reflect the relationship of supply and demand, conform to the law which governs market economy and ensures the normal clearance of market. Market clearing means the actual possibility of free trading between local and foreign currencies. Therefore, the theory of monetary convertibility is that of the rationalization of an exchange rate.

Generally put, dual exchange rate has always existed in the socialist economies and developing economies. That is the overvaluation of local currency, which is related to the development strategies of import substitution and the arbitrary pricing in a planned economy. In the regime of highly twisted pricing, not only does a dual exchange rate exists, but also multiple exchange rates need to be practised. To realise an equilibrium exchange rate, what is to be done first is to enforce a price reform, put an end to the strategies of economic development of import substitution, and change it into the neutral trade policy of balancing import substitution with export leading. The two basic conditions constitute the premise to the rationalization of exchange rate.

2) Convertibility of Currency Calls for Government Commitment and Confidence of the Public

In the regime of overvaluation of local currency, people are willing to convert their local currency at the official exchange rate into foreign currency and bide their time to exchange it back for local one from the adjustment market to increase the value of their own currency. If their motives were assumed as unchanged activities, then the realization of monetary convertibility must entail sufficient reserve of foreign currency, a strong capacity of export and comprehensive national strength. Only in this way can residents and enterprises' demand for foreign exchange be met. This assumption is actually wrong, and the tendency actually is not in existence under the conditions of rationalization of exchange rate. If the government gives the commitment that the local currency may be converted into foreign currency at any time, it will make residents believe that the local currency and foreign exchange are equal in value at a certain exchange rate and that people have no need to convert the local currency into foreign one or to do so in haste.

Another reason of hard currency holding is that people think that it has a value-keeping character and it can guard against domestic inflation. Therefore, to keep a low inflation rate is important to the regime of convertible currency. But even if under the unfortunate circumstances of a fairly high rate of inflation, if the government can compile the price index statistics according to the actual conditions, perform the positive real interest rates and infuse a knowledge of the steadfastness and consistency of this policy to the people, then, to exchange the savings of local currency plus the interest accrued for foreign currency will leave the value of the assets of the real currency unchanged. After the government has given this commitment, its residents will build a confidence in their local currency. The resumption of the confidence in the currency means a change in the previous conduct and the cure for high-rising inflation. Experience has shown that the commitment of the government will change the rules of the conduct. It is superficial to allege that sufficient foreign exchange reserve must be available to cope with the conversion so as to realize the convertibility of currency.

Modern economic theory emphasizes very much study of the roles of commitment. Government bonds, contracts, laws and rules and regulations are the manifestations of commitment. The general practice is to maintain this commitment, and any violation must be corrected to uphold the rules of activities. Government commitment is important and the commitment can trim the circumscription of economic activities to some extent and the conduct beyond circumvention is accidental and must be handled accordingly. The government can establish new regulations in the form of laws and rules and fulfil the fresh commitments it makes.

The confidence of the public in the local currency will affect their confidence in the politics and economy in their own country. A strong confidence in local currency actually embodies the steady growth and prosperity of the local economy. In case of insufficient confidence in local currency people will play down psychologically the local commodities and services, holding that foreign currencies are hard, and their technology, quality of services are good and, foreign goods are genuine and their prices reasonable. This tendency will lead to an underestimation of the whole national economy and a lack of confidence in it.

2. Requirements of Opening-up Policy for Convertibility of Currency

According to experts, the open-up policy advocates more participation in international division of labour, and in competition of international market, including permission for participation by international trade partners in domestic competition. To develop outwardly-oriented economy calls for the convertibility of currency, or else it will bring about a series of problems.

The advantages of free convertibility of currency are: non-convertibility of currency of a nation will narrow the scope of its multilateral trade. To allow the currency to be convertible will be conducive to the exchanges of commodities and labour service with other countries. Therefore, people call a freely convertible currency, a mechanism of free price and operational autonomy of enterprises three major factors of market economy. The inconvertibility of currency hinders the import of foreign investment, the overseas investment by domestic businesses and triggers the outflow of foreign exchange. To exercise the free convertibility of currency will be helpful in solving the imbalance in the supply of and demand for foreign exchange, and any deficiency in foreign exchange in particular. While exercising foreign exchange control by other means will cost much and cause a poor efficiency of fund employment and, the co-existence of multiple exchange rates will prompt "lease hunting". Realizing free convertibility of currency can slash overhead expenses, increase the utilization rate of foreign exchange and curtail the opportunity of "lease setting-up" and "lease hunting".

China provides that Renminbi is a domestic circulating currency and no free conversion is permitted, nor can any foreign currency be used inside China. Trading currency without permission is in violation of the regulations for foreign exchange control. Dual exchange rate has meanwhile been conducted on official and adjustment markets. Since different exporters have enjoyed the treatment of different percentage of foreign exchange retention, for the part of exporters, multiple exchange rates have actually existed. Similar cases have been seen in the fields of foreign exchange earning not through trade.

The inconvertibility of currency tends to be accompanied by overvaluation of local currency and shortage of foreign exchange. The effect of overvaluing local currency is the encouragement of imports and restrictions on exports, therefore, foreign exchange is bound to fall short. The shorter the foreign exchange falls, the more dependence there is on administrative methods equalizing foreign exchange and the more unacceptable it will be to let the market evaluate the currency. The result is: the overvaluation of local currency tends to remain unchanged. Under the circumstances, to attract direct investment of foreign businesses, it is necessary that foreign-funded enterprises strike a balance between RMB and foreign exchange and find a solution to foreign exchange in many other occasions by themselves, prompting more restrictions on the choice of their industries and more inconvenience in management.

In trade, overvaluation of local currency and inconvertibility of currency discriminate exports, but is favourable to the policy of import protection, hence it impedes a nation from being more fully involved in international division of labour. As exports fail to play a big role, less foreign exchange is earned, which restricts the extent of exchange utilizing for imports. Besides, the adoption of development strategies of import substitution means to import technical equipment and other imports with foreign exchange at lower prices to encourage import substitution industries. This brings about the overvaluation of local currency in the developing and socialist countries, and loss sustained by the exporter for the exchange settlement every time he exports one US dollar (or other hard currencies) worth of commodities. Hence the exporter has to choose high profit-earning products or those subsidised by the state for export, and thereby export capacity fails to develop fully. In connection with this, great profit has been earned in imports. And the excessive profit earning leads to the administrative control, which makes the scarce foreign exchange used only in areas in which the state wants to import. On the other hand, the state does not permit the import of what it thinks is nonessential. This hinders the effect and expension of the advantages of free decision making in the micro-economy, especially disadvantageous to the diversified development of production and consumption.

The inconvertibility of currency also has an impact on the flow of capital. The flow of capital involves foreign-business direct investment and financing in the form of debt. The overvaluation of local currency will inevitably affect the calculation of shares by foreign businessmen who make investments in equity joint ventures in China, hence it is directly concerned with the rights and interests of foreign investors. Owing to currency inconvertibility, restrictions to some extent are placed on the outward remittance of foreign exchange under different items of payments in foreign-funded enterprises. In debt financing, only a few corporations or banks enjoying the trust of the state are allowed to do so. Sometimes, it is simply in the name of the state to make debt financing from other countries.

In capital outflow, foreign exchange outflow is generally restricted because of the shortage of foreign currencies in developing and socialist countries. It stands to reason that, to improve "North"-"South" economic relations, capital should flow from developed countries to developing countries, but the U.S. statistics show that the outflow of the capital from China to the U.S. was more than the inflow from the U.S. to China, and the outflow appeared in a not very clear form. To conduct currency convertibility will obviously play a monitoring role in capital outflow and the tendency of capital inflow will be augmented, thus facilitating the balance of international payment. The examples in some Latin American countries demonstrate the phenomenon well. In carrying out development strategies of import substitution, the countries all adopted protective practices. Their exports not being strong, they exercised control of foreign exchange with irrational exchange rates and at the same time borrowed large sums of foreign money, hence slow growth in their economies occurred, resulting in a huge capital outflow. In the wake of a series of recent reforms, inflation has been curbed, the exchange rate made rational, trade deregulated, and less control of capital flow made the capital, which drained away enormously, flow back a great deal.

In short, a regime of convertible currency must be carried out if a country wants to go towards open market economy.

3. Background of China's Reform of Exchange Rate System

Given the current economic growth in China, what should be the actual condition under which the system of a unitary exchange rate rationally reflecting the economic activities on the market can be set up and Renminbi made freely convertible?

Some experts hold that from the angle of macro-economy, the basic feature in economic reform of the 1980s in China was to introduce a market mechanism. In the 1990s, in step with the deepening of the economic reform and opening-up, the market mechanism is moving towards maturity, offering a motive force to the economic growth.

As far as the system of exchange control is concerned, an important symbol of introducing and establishing the market mechanism during the 1980s is foreign exchange adjustment between domestic businesses, beginning from October, 1980. The development during the following decade saw the market of foreign exchange adjustment going through a process from establishment to maturity.

The market has passed through a process from adjustment by the Bank of China to the establishment of specialised foreign exchange markets in provinces, municipalities and autonomous regions across the nation and their participation in the adjustment.

The market of foreign exchange adjustment evolved from the adoption of cash adjustment into that of the co-existence of cash adjustment and the quota one.

Price adjustment has been through a process of gradual deregulation. At the beginning of the adjustment operation, it was provided that on the basis of the price of internal settlement of trade foreign exchange (one US dollar equalled 2.8 RMB yuan), the price of foreign exchange adjustment had a ceiling of one US dollar against 3.08 RMB yuan, that is, adding a range of 10 percent floating.

The trading volume grows incessantly. The adjustment of foreign exchange increased from several hundred million US dollars in 1980 to 8.566 billion US dollars in 1988 and further to more than 10 billion US dollars in 1990.

China's market of foreign exchange adjustment has grown somewhat with the introduction of mechanism of market economy. Nevertheless, it has still failed to develop in tandem with the economic growth in China.

1) Large Limitations Remain in the Range of Foreign Exchange Adjustment

Many residents and individual economic units cannot yet participate in foreign exchange adjustment. Even if in the places where markets for the adjustment of individual foreign exchange were available, too strict requirements governing individuals' participation in adjustment are in place. The price of foreign exchange adjustment is fixed fairly low, and only exchange selling but not buying is allowed. This has no doubt curbed the inflow of overseas Chinese remittances and other foreign exchange, and has encouraged trading on the black markets. This is very unfavourable to the growth of the market of foreign exchange adjustment. Apart from this, influence of domestic local protectionism causes the phenomenon that adjustment of foreign exchange has been blocked from one another in various regions. It is evidenced that when foreign exchange is in big demand, administrative measures are there to limit the outflow of foreign exchange; while the market slackens, the inflow of foreign exchange from other localities is restricted. Consequently, the inter-regional adjustment of foreign exchange has been hampered severely, affecting the rational flow of foreign exchange funds and weakening the competitive mechanism of market. Meanwhile, the market of foreign exchange adjustment has not changed the status quo of the multi-tiered exchange rate system in China.

As far as China is concerned, the aim of the reform of the system of RMB exchange rate is to realize fully the free convertibility of RMB and the establishment of the system of floating exchange rate to make it highly liberalized and internationalized. In the near future, the first thing to do is to realize the free conversion of RMB within the country. In other words, on the basis of unified and wholly liberalized domestic market of foreign exchange, RMB exchange rate will make a transition from the multi-tier system of the co-existence of official exchange rate, that of adjustment market and that of the black market to the system of unified and unitary exchange rate. The official exchange rate will no longer be quoted and only the exchange rate for reference is there to be seen. The exchange rate will be decided upon by the relationship between supply and demand on the foreign exchange market. The state will make adjustment from the macro economic angle such as intervention in foreign exchange markets, capital managements, and monetary policies inclusive of interest rate, discount rate and legal deposit requirements. If the treasury bonds can grow to hit the level of the issuance of treasury bills of the U.S., the state can influence the psychology of dealings by the public so as to affect and manage the exchange rate indirectly by intervening in the stock market and quoting the exchange rate of reference. It can thus make the rate fluctuate around the target of exchange rate within a modest range. This is also the experience in exchange rate control in a great majority of countries worldwide. It can undoubtedly be used by us. The combination of indirect intervention by the government and the regulation of the market feature in the exchange rate system in economically developed countries worldwide. No country on the globe is free in exchange rate floating. The well-known are the systems of exchange rate control of the "snake in the tunnel" of EEC and of the "small snake in the tunnel" used by Holland, Belgium and Luxembourg in EEC.

From the present conditions of China, to match with the system, foreign exchange control must continue to be deregulated to let all businesses and individuals at home buy and sell foreign currencies in RMB freely, i.e., to realize the free conversion of RMB domestically and, within a not too long period of time, RMB should become freely exchangeable internationally. This short-term target is likely to enter a trial stage. Because basic conditions are available in China already: a. Its economy and finance has been opened wider. In 1992, China's ratio of outwardly-oriented trade to the total national output value amounted to 19.3 percent, higher than the exporter power of Japan, the value of export-import trade constitutes 36 percent of the GNP, the value of exports reached 71.9 billion US dollars, becoming the 13th largest export country in the world. In recent years, the number of foreign-funded enterprises increased year by year with a total of more than 30,000 and the investment by foreign businesses exceeded 80 billion US dollars and more and more foreign consortiums and financial institutions have joined the rank. b. The reform of foreign trade system has been fruitful with the mix of export commodities further improved, the growth of outwardly-oriented economy gaining momentum and the competitive capacity of Chinese goods on international market increasing greatly. c. Thanks to the good balance of international payments, China's foreign exchange reserve is growing year by year, with year-end figure of 28.59 billion US dollars in 1990 and 42.66 billion US dollars in 1991, up 49.2 percent. d. The market of foreign exchange adjustment has taken shape and grown rather rapidly, and is developing gradually to an advanced level.

2) Domestic and International Markets of Foreign Exchange Needed in the Trial Stage of the Short-Term Target

With the gradual development in breadth and depth of the export-oriented economy, the foreign exchange market shall tend towards the international standard, forming a two-tier structure: Tier one is the domestic market of foreign exchange. Its basic function is to realize the mutual conversion between the local currency, namely RMB, and foreign currencies, so it can also be called money exchange market. Tier two is the international market of foreign exchange which will dovetail with the international one so as to handle the trade between different foreign currencies. It will function as follows: a. the role of settlement: it serves as the means of payment and of settlement in international economic transactions to realize the free transfer of purchasing power without any limitations of national boundaries; b. the role in financing and circulation of capital; c. the role of risk avoidance. In the foreign exchange market, spot exchange can be conducted, and more important, the forward trade be carried out with hedging to evade the risk brought about by the change in exchange rates.

The free conversion of local currency is the most basic condition for setting up foreign exchange market according to international standards. Only when RMB becomes a freely exchangeable currency, can RMB vs. foreign currencies and one foreign currency vs. another one be freely converted in China, can international capital flow in and out of China freely and can a real international market of foreign exchange be set up.

From the history of the economic growth of the newly industrialized countries of the world, an important signal of their economic takeoff is that when conditions are ripe, control of foreign exchange is removed, local and foreign currencies can be traded freely and the free foreign exchange market be set up.

4. Premises of RMB Becoming a Freely Convertible Currency

1) To Set up Foreign Exchange Equalization Fund to Gorge and Disgorge Amounts in Foreign Exchange, Regulate Foreign Exchange Balance and Stabilize Prices of Foreign Exchange to Keep the Exchange Rate Comparatively Stable.

A special amount in the foreign exchange equalization fund can be appropriated by the central bank for the portion in terms of RMB and the portion in foreign exchange set aside from the state reserve of foreign exchange. It is worth our study that the Hong Kong government sets up a foreign exchange fund to stabilize the exchange rate of Hong Kong dollar. According to the statistics issued by the Hong Kong government in July, 1992, Hong Kong's foreign exchange fund at the year-end of 1991 stood at 236 billion US dollars, the foreign currency reserve among the foreign exchange fund at 29 billion US dollars, ranking 12th in the world with per capita holdings of 5,000 US dollars. One of the important reasons accounting for the rapid economic growth of Hong Kong in the 1980s was the system of the rate pegged to the US dollar on the premise of a huge foreign exchange fund. China's foreign exchange reserve amounted to 42.66 billion US dollars at the end of 1991. Since China is adhering to the existent reform and open policy, its foreign exchange reserve registered 31.4 billion US dollars at the end of June, 1994.

In reality, China's outwardly-oriented economy has attained a new height with a growing momentum and steadily increasing foreign exchange reserve. This provides a solid foundation for establishing a foreign exchange equalization fund in China aiming at stabilizing RMB exchange rate. By the end of 1991, the Bank of China's rank rose to the 22nd position from the 30th in 1990 among the world leading banks.

2) Subject RMB to Proper Devaluation

From the practice of the economic takeoff of outwardly-oriented economy in most developing countries, at the stage that economy started to grow rapidly, a sweeping reform was effected first in the exchange rate system, and the devaluation of the local currency against foreign currencies is always the prelude to the reform of the exchange rate system. Since the stage of fast growth of export-oriented economy is also in the export-leading economic period, it is always preceded by an import substitution period. The overvaluation of local currency against foreign ones features in the exchange rate system over a period of import substitution. An exchange rate characterized by the overvaluation local currency plays the role of encouraging import substitution. While entering export-leading period, to devaluate the local currency properly in due course and change the exchange rate of previously over-valued local currency into a real one formed through the supply and demand of market is beneficial to the promotion of the international competitiveness of the export-leading economy and can play the role of stimulating exports.

There remains some controversy as to whether proper devaluation of the exchange rate of RMB in China at present can raise international competitiveness to promote export growth.

Those against devaluation hold that using the approach of devaluation of local currency to boost outwardly-oriented economy entails certain premises, of which the most important is that the conditions of elasticity of international trade must be offered, that is, it shall satisfy the Marshall-Lerner Condition: the elasticity of supply of the commodities of import and export are all infinite, the sum of the absolute value of the elasticity of demand of the import and export commodities must be bigger than one.

The arguments and conclusion drawn by those opposing the proper devaluation of RMB against foreign currencies do not correspond to the objective reality provided by China's reform and opening-up over the decade. According to the estimation by some experts, the elasticity of the price of demand for imports in China was about -0.35, while that for exports -0.86, the sum of the absolute value of both was bigger than one. Moreover, China began to regulate the exchange rate on October 30, 1985, down to one US dollar against 3.32 RMB yuan and several devaluations ensued in a row. The official rate is one US dollar against 5.44 RMB yuan at the end of 1990, and against 8.58 RMB yuan in August, 1994. In step with the downward value of RMB against foreign currencies, China's foreign trade-oriented economy has achieved fast growth.

The rapid growth of China's outwardly-oriented economy and its increasing demand for participation in integrating with the international economy has revealed that the existent exchange rate system in China does not meet the needs of the outwardly-oriented economic development. It departs from the real supply and demand conditions of market and is bound to bring about an unusual twist of efficiency in the rational allocation of the scarce resources of foreign exchange and derange the resources allocation according to the economic principle. To find a solution to the puzzle of the outwardly-oriented economic growth, people must make the existent exchange rate of RMB against foreign currencies conform to the requirements of markets.

5. The Supporting Reform and Design of RMB Going to Convertible Currency

1) To Realize a Rational Exchange Rate

The rational point of exchange rate is the equilibrium rate which maintains the balance of international payments in support of RMB becoming a convertible currency. To realize the equilibrium rate of exchange entails two approaches, one is that the official authorities set the exchange rate at the point of equilibrium by computation; the other is that the equilibrium rate is decided upon by market clearance through realization of full foreign exchange retention by exporters to open the market of foreign exchange or of document of retention. The exchange rate tending towards rationalization will change the way foreign exchange is distributed by a wide margin, thus spurring on the promotion of the efficiency of resources allocation of the whole society. Two technically different transitional paths are available compared to the two approaches to realizing the equilibrium rate of exchange. Export and import, which hold main status in the payments and receipts of foreign exchange in China, shall be taken as the basic starting point of fixing the scheme of exchange rate regulation.

2) To Conduct Management of Aggregate Demand

It is hard to effect economic reform in an unstable economic environment under inflation, therefore the management of aggregate demand is the prerequisite of reform and of all other economic policies. The practice of the rectification of economic environment from 1988 onward has proved the necessity and feasibility of exercising the management of aggregate demand. However owing to the use of some administrative interference, cases of enterprises being injured have arisen. This can be attributed to incomplete experience and knowledge in combating inflation in the environment of a fairly developing commodity economy for the first time. Economic theory or international experience all show that there is a package of more accurate and effective policies of anti-inflation with less side-effects.

Another approach for inflation control in recent years is to change the local currency categorically into the convertible and use the commitment of the government to breed the confidence of the public in the local currency. In spite of the state's insufficient reserve of foreign exchange, this change is least likely to send people hurrying to convert local currency into foreign currencies blindly, or produce an adverse impact on the state's reserve of foreign exchange.

3) Reform of Price

The reform of price is one of the most important fundamental issues of economic structural reforms in socialist countries, as in the practice of China's economic restructuring.

The significance of an equilibrium price is to make the price the correct signal in resources allocation so as to realize optimal resources allocation of Pareto, thus increasing the economic efficiency markedly and providing a motivating force for economic development and the deepening of reform. The course of price reform is classified into several different stages and the formation of the system of equilibrium price has to pass through a course of gradual formation. In some links of yet premature mechanism, such as the capital market and futures market, it is unlikely that the price reaches a stable state of equilibrium once it becomes liberalized due to the still imperfect supporting organizational setup. In achieving an equilibrium price, the approach to price adjustment is not ruled out. Equilibrium here not only refers to the equilibrium of supply and demand of one commodity, it is also concerned with the inter-influences among products of many departments and the inter-influences formed in the combination and changes of the production factors, that is, the general equilibrium of the whole system of products and various factors of production.

4) Reform of Structure of Foreign Trade

To abandon the mandatory plan of export, separate the functions of government from those of enterprises and to set up a new system of regulation: a. Rationalization of exchange rate; b. The whole drawback of indirect tax on exports and duty on imports (including the duty on indirect imports); c. Credit support should be lent to the export industries with comparative advantages conforming to development strategies in China; d. To improve the effectiveness and uniformity of duty regulation, reduce the administrative examination and approval, and narrow discrepancies in the rates of duty; e. Bid-inviting or auction shall be conducted regarding the necessary quota of imports and exports to improve the fairness of distribution of the quota and to embody the principle of priority of economic efficiency. f. To minimise direct interference from administrative departments and put into effect the operational power of enterprises.

5) Reform in Direct Investment by Foreign Businesses

To perfect and further amend legislation, abandon compulsory self-balance in foreign exchange so as to make foreign investment choose the market more freely. Excepting the formulation of concise and feasible legislation concerning foreign-funded enterprises and the reform of environment of investment, to reform the regime of exchange rate and speed up the course of convertibility of currency have become very important measures. The excessive inter-regional policy differences are unfair and to implement the policy of all-dimensional opening is beneficial to the optimization of the whole situation of resources allocation.

6) Concerning System of Planning and Industrial Policy

The role of planning should be reserved to a certain extent in the link with external effects in respect of infrastructural facilities, in the link of the scale efficiency being remarkable and monopolies of natural resources being in existence. But the role of planning should further be reduced in other respects and especially in normal productive fields. The policy of industry should be led appropriately through economic leverage and economic interests and a tiny minority of departments should adopt some prohibitive practices. First, the development of a market mechanism should be perfected so that the mechanism can take the lead in resources allocation; meanwhile the imperfect allocation by market of resources should be recognized and the government should make appropriate regulations a priority through the policy of industry. Trade should be universally promoted and the growth of outwardly-oriented economy propelled.

7) Concerning Foreign Exchange System

The practices in most Western industrialized countries and developing countries indicate that there are two ways to approach the rationalization of exchange rate. One is that only the local currency is permitted to go current domestically and the exchange of all proceeds must be settled immediately upon export. It is free to buy exchange if only the contract of import is available. The other approach permits no exchange settlement after export and the exchange rate is decided upon by the foreign exchange market so that the exchange proceeds of export can be channelled into the hands of the importer. If an inference is made from the development and postponement of the system of foreign exchange retention in China, exporters should be permitted to obtain 100 percent retention and the rate of foreign exchange be formed through the foreign exchange market. The planned foreign exchange used in such as the administration and the public expenditures of foreign exchange of embassies abroad and in the national defence shall be bought back at a rational exchange rate. The foreign exchange market allows the rationalization of the exchange rate to be realized through exchange trading. Another approach is that the official authority sets a rational exchange rate and requires that exchange from exportation must be settled. Since the exchange rate is rational and unitary, and exchange purchase is permitted, this actually amounts to 100 percent foreign exchange retention. It shall be exercised that all exporters settle their proceeds of exchange, and permission be given to exchange buying for all the demands under the items of current account, and a current exchange rate be floated by the official authority according to the information available, thus making the rate fall basically at the equilibrium point. The rate may be subject to the decision of the interbank market. The central bank can intervene in short-term fluctuations of the exchange rate but it should not imagine subjectively a level of exchange rate while in more occasions the market shall play a role instead.

It may be considered that exchange control can be lifted in two steps and ultimately the free convertibility of Renminbi realized. As a first step, the convertibility shall be realised under the current account, mainly to lift foreign exchange restrictions on international trade, labour co-operation and technical import under the current account. Then after a period of time, the decontrol may be further extended to capital outflow and the non-trade exchange of the residents. To realize convertibility of currency is a rather big step and all the influences produced thereby should be analyzed clearly. The motive for the prompt realization of convertibility of currency is mainly to curb high inflation. While the inflation rate in China is not high, the requirements in this respect is not pressing. From this angle, to proceed by two steps can ascertain the actual conditions and accumulate experience, thus making the second step more secure. After the decontrol of foreign exchange at the second step, a foreign exchange market with a high-level of freedom can be set up.

6. The Influence of Conducting Currency Convertibility

According to experts, the advantages of practising convertibility of currency are:

First, it is favourable to the improvement of the balance of receipts and outlays of foreign exchange and to the promotion of the shift of a mix of commodities for export. The adjustment of exchange rate will yield the normal profit from exports, develop the initiative of the enterprises of export, increase the import cost and effect a curbing role on imports of high elasticity. The increase of exports and the decrease in imports will facilitate the balance of international payments. It can also play an active role in objectively appraising the operational performance of enterprises of foreign trade, straightening out economic relations and overcoming the imbalance of grief and joy among the enterprises.

Second, it is favourable to the betterment of fiscal revenues and expenditures. In the wake of the depreciation of RMB, corresponding changes have effected the mix of exports and imports. Export production can be enlarged and employment and fiscal revenues increased, in tandem with the subsidies called for in the rate of customs duties. The portion of foreign debts borne by the government has entailed more RMB funds for exchange buying to effect debt service. The adjustment of fiscal revenues and expenditures will be helpful to their balance.

Third, the relationship between the adjustment of the exchange rate and inflation. The imbalance of trade can be removed in two ways: the depreciation of the exchange rate accompanied by other economic levers; direct control is imposed on part of foreign trade and foreign exchange. Both ways result in the promotion of exports and restrictions on imports, widening the gap of domestic demand and supply, creating an inflationary rate with modest difference of quantity but with different effects on the mix of imports and exports and on the structure of pricing. The administrative method plays a big role in enlarging the export of primary products, so does the adjustment of the exchange rate in expanding exports of diversified manufactured products. Since the mix of consumption of the residents in China has a bigger dependence on primary products, it will exert more influence on the consumption index in the administrative vehicles, while the adoption of economic vehicles will be favourable to straightening out economic relations. The inflation rate brought about by indirect control as a means of regulating the exchange rate is lower.

Fourth, the relations between the adjustment of exchange rate and the foreign exchange earnings of non-trade. The proper depreciation of RMB will not decrease the earnings of foreign exchange of non-trade. The situation with the banknote in lieu of exchange and materials in lieu of exchange as prompted by the overvaluation of Renminbi will be ameliorated, and overseas Chinese remittances are likely to increase.

Fifth, the relationship between the adjustment of foreign exchange and the introduction of foreign capital. The influence exerted by RMB depreciation on the net inflow of foreign capital is on the whole beneficial. The equity capital of direct foreign investment of equal amounts will be enlarged conspicuously and the capital returns of foreign investment increase obviously, which is a favourable influence on the net inflow of foreign capital. For foreign capital already introduced, the gains of foreign capital in foreign-funded enterprises will increase.

In addition, it is necessary to further clarify the influences on issue on exercising convertibility of currency.

First, the influence on the overall level of pricing. The implementation of the adjustment of exchange rate will surely exert an influence on the price structure, but the effect on the overall level of pricing involves choices of several important hypotheses and their testing and verification: a. Under the management of aggregate demand, the adjustment of the exchange rate will bring about the comparative adjustment of interests; b. To measure the demand elasticity, supply elasticity and substitution elasticity of the different economic entities for foreign exchange in the real economic environment. c. The adjustment of the exchange rate will improve the efficiency of the distribution of foreign exchange resources and the improvement of resources allocation will bring about the increase of the GNP and fiscal revenue. The several premises are vital, involving the basic understanding of the economic structural reform. They are the basic assessment of current national conditions in China and the starting point for the design of supporting policies. If the exchange rate is adjusted soberly and consciously, and the aggregate demand is meanwhile brought under strict control, the adjustment of the exchange rate will bring along mainly changes in the comparative price rather than in the total level of pricing.

Second, the effect on the protective policy. It is worth conscientiously considering whether China needs full-range and all-trade industries. A complete range of industries indicates that the strength of the state is strong and does not need depend on foreign countries. In fact, it is unnecessary to hold this position in the current world. Meanwhile, trade protectionism will make society defray all kinds of costs. The cost of efficiency may be classified into loss of consumption and loss of production. The former refers to loss in the real income of the consumer from protected products, loss which is incurred by the trade protection which drives the consumer to pay a higher price; the producers benefit from the higher prices and tend to increase output. The latter denotes that the resources, which would be used otherwise in economic activities (including the production for the export), will be taken out to be put in this production, while the resources used otherwise may be more efficient. In addition, loss in connection with the so-called x inefficiency is likely to occur.

Third, regarding capital flow, trade proceeds and outlays. Under the circumstances of an irrational exchange rate or foreign exchange control, the flight of a large amount of capital is bound to occur. At present many people are making the transfer outwardly in irregular and covert methods. Statistics cannot be compiled as to just how much capital is being drained. Once the currency becomes exchangeable, the normal remittance of funds may be made through the public channel. With the exchange rate made rationalized and the public having more confidence in the local currency, the capital outflow will be reduced to some extent and the inflow of capital will increase. The capital outflow is also connected to the economic growth and conditions. If the reform and the opening-up is accelerated, inclusive of currency convertibility, the deregulation of trade operation, pricing to be decided on by supply-and-demand conditions on the market and a promising vista opened to domestic economic growth, the capital will certainly flow back.

In short, the positive role of currency convertibility is certain. The conclusion is that reform should be speeded up with firmer steps in this direction.

图书在版编目（CIP）数据

中国金融体制改革：英文/高尚全，迟福林主编；朱华友执笔.
—北京：外文出版社，1996
（中国市场经济研讨/外文出版社主编）
ISBN 7‐119‐01341‐6

Ⅰ.中⋯ Ⅱ.①高⋯ ②迟⋯ ③朱⋯ Ⅲ.金融体制‐经济体制改革
‐中国‐英文 Ⅳ.F832.1

中国版本图书馆 CIP 数据核字（95）第 09629 号

中国金融体制改革

高尚全　迟福林　主编

朱华友　执笔

*

ⓒ外文出版社

外文出版社出版

（中国北京百万庄路 24 号）

邮政编码 100037

北京外文印刷厂印刷

中国国际图书贸易总公司发行

（中国北京车公庄西路 35 号）

北京邮政信箱第 399 号　邮政编码 100044

1996 年（大 32 开）第一版

（英）

ISBN 7‐119‐01341‐6 /F·35（外）

02100

4‐E‐2937P

3986 028

mc